GCSE English
for AQA B

John Law • David Stone

Heinemann

Heinemann Educational Publishers
Halley Court, Jordan Hill, Oxford OX2 8EJ
Part of Harcourt Education Limited

Heinemann is a registered trademark of
Harcourt Education Limited

Text © John Law and David Stone 2002

First published in 2002

06 05
10 9 8 7 6 5 4 3 2

ISBN 0 435 10605 8

Copyright notice

Produced by Start to Finish
Original illustrations © Reed Educational & Professional Publishing Ltd 2002
Illustrations by Linda Jeffrey and Ruth Palmer
Design: Cover: Wooden Ark. Inside: Paul Manning
Printed and bound in the UK by Bath Colourbooks

Acknowledgements

The authors and publishers are grateful to the following for permission to reproduce previously published material:

Atlantic Syndication: for Alex Brummer, 'Yes, but is it the last hurrah of the boom?' from *Mail on Sunday* (30 December 2001); Matthew Bond, 'Epic Wizardry and all the Rest' from *Mail on Sunday* (16 December 2001); Rebecca English and Peter Markham, 'We've spent £15 billion' from *Daily Mail* (28 December 2001); Robert Hardman, 'In the Retail Temple, worshipping frantically' from *Mail on Sunday* (30 December 2001); **Marion Boyars Publishers:** for Kath Walker, 'Bwalla the Hunter' from *The Dawn Is At Hand: Selected Poems* (Marion Boyars, 1992); **Bristol Evening Post:** for Simon Peevers, 'Cash-Happy Hordes Fill City Shops' from *Evening Post* (28 December 2001); **Faber & Faber Ltd:** from Alan Bennett, *Writing Home* (Faber & Faber, 1994); **Guardian Newspapers Ltd:** for 'A wounded world: America's pain was felt across the globe' from *The Guardian* (31 December 2001), © Guardian; 'Big freeze sets in for the New Year' from *The Guardian* (30 December 2001), © Guardian; Vivek Chaudhary, 'Why football may stay at home' from *The Guardian*, © Guardian; Tom Robbins, 'Britain shivers at end of record-breaking warm year' from *The Guardian*, © Guardian; **Hippopotamus Press:** for A.L. Hendriks, 'The Fringe of the Sea' from *To Speak Simply: Selected Poems 1961–1986* (Hippopotamus Press, 1986); **Macmillan, London:** from Julian Barnes, *Something to Declare* (Picador, 2001); from Jane Lapotaire, *Grace and Favour* (Macmillan, 1989); from John Simpson, *A Mad World, My Masters* (Macmillan, 2000); **News International Newspapers Ltd:** for 'Spending for victory' from *Sunday Times* (30 December 2001), © Times Newspapers Ltd, London, 2001; Margarette Driscoll and Jane Mulkerrins, 'Shopping: it's a guy thing' from *The Sunday Times* (30 December 2001), © Times Newspapers Ltd, London, 2001; Gillian Harris and Adam Fresco, 'Snow and gales cut power and cause chaos' from *The Sunday Times* (30 December 2001), © Times Newspapers Ltd, London, 2001; Russell Jenkins and Linus Gregoriadis, 'Gales sweep in after snowfalls' from *The Times* (26 January 2002), © Times Newspapers Ltd, London, 2002; Paul Simons, 'When the weather goes like a bomb' from *The Times* (2 February 2002), © Paul Simons/Times Newspapers Ltd, London, 2002; Tim Teeman, 'Flooding alerts rise as storms sweep in' from *The Times* (2 February 2002), © Times Newspapers Ltd, London, 2002; **Orion Publishing Group and Curtis Brown Ltd:** for Li Bai, 'The Road to Shu is Hard', translated by Vikram Seth, from *Three Chinese Poets*, edited by Vikram Seth (Phoenix, 1997); **Peter Owen Ltd, London:** for George Awoonor-Williams, 'The Sea Eats the Land at Home', reprinted in *Emergency Kit*, edited by Jo Shapcott and Matthew Sweeney (Faber & Faber, 1996); **People & Planet:** for text adapted from www.peopleandplanet.org website; **The Scotsman Publications Ltd:** for 'Darkness at heart of consumer spending spree' from *The Scotsman* (28 December 2001), adapted from www.thescotsman.co.uk website; **Serpent's Tail Press:** for John Agard, 'Palm Tree King' from *Mangoes and Bullets* (Serpent's Tail, 1990); **Shetland Islands Tourism:** for text adapted from www.visitshetland.com website; **Sunday Independent:** for Kirsty Turner, 'Boy, 14, saves woman as car is swept away' from *Sunday Independent* (3 February 2002); **Telegraph Group Ltd:** for Hamida Ghafour, 'Gales bring flooding and power cuts' from *The Daily Telegraph* (2 February, 2002), © Telegraph Group Ltd, 2002; **Transworld Publishers:** from Bill Bryson, *Neither Here Nor There: Travels in Europe* (Black Swan, 1998), © Bill Bryson. All rights reserved; The Vegetarian Society: for text adapted from www.vegsoc.org website.

Every effort has been made to trace or contact all copyright holders. The publishers would be pleased to rectify any omissions brought to their notice at the earliest opportunity.

The publishers would like to thank the following for permission to reproduce photographs: **Action-Plus/Neil Tingle** p.88; **Atlantic Syndication** p.5 (inset); **John Birdsall Photography** p.39; **The Ronald Grant Archive** p.136; **Peter Macdiarmid** p.44 right; **Murdo Mcleod** p.27; **NI Syndication/The Sunday Times/Francesco Guidicini** p.26; **NI Syndication/The Times/Chris Harris** p.38 bottom; **North News & Pictures** p.5 (background); **PA Photos/Owen Humphries** p.37 left; **PA Photos/Paul Faith** pp37 right & 38 top; **PA Photos/Ben Curtis** p.40; **PA Photos/John Giles** p.45; **Solent News** p.44 left; **South West News Service/Rowan Griffiths** p.8; **Still Moving Picture Library/David Robertson** p.97 left & right; **Still Moving Picture Library/Ken Paterson** p.98 bottom; **Still Moving Picture Library/David Robertson** p.98 top; **Still Pictures/Paul Gipe** p.80; **Still Pictures/Dera** p.130; **Courtesy of The Vegetarian Society** p.93.

Tel: 01865 888058   www.heinemann.co.uk

Contents

Introduction

GCSE English for AQA B will help you to achieve your best possible grade in the AQA English, Specification B examination and build your confidence. Its aim is to ensure that you are fully prepared for both papers:

- *Paper 1*
  Section A: Reading media texts and non-fiction texts
  Section B: Writing to argue, persuade, advise
- *Paper 2*
  Section A: Reading poetry from different cultures and traditions
  Section B: Writing to analyse, review, comment.

The book is designed to help you to develop the particular skills which are tested in the examination – reading and writing. Although intended to be of use to all students, those likely to gain most from working through this examination-centred book are candidates in the middle range, at grade C.

Many students ask: How do I prepare for the examination? The problem is that, unlike most examinations, there is no actual content to be revised for this exam – there are no facts or formulae to be learned, no dates or names to be memorised. What you need to do is to practise the skills of reading and writing. You will already be doing this in the classroom as you produce your coursework assignments, but this book prepares you precisely for the kinds of questions you are going to find on the examination papers.

As you work your way through the book – with your teacher in the classroom, or completing homework assignments – you will be practising these skills. On the day you walk into the examination room you should be ready for anything.

About the authors

John Law teaches at St Anselm's Catholic School, Canterbury, and David Stone teaches at The Grange Community School, South Gloucestershire. Both are experienced examiners.

How to use this book

This book offers a step-by-step approach to your GCSE English examination, and will build up your confidence. It begins with the first question on Paper 1 and ends with the last question on Paper 2. It is probably best, though not essential, to work through the book chapter by chapter.

Each examination question is approached in a series of steps, as you will see below – you begin with example questions or modelled pieces of writing and are given plenty of help. The help is then gradually withdrawn as you progress through the *Practice* sections, until you are able to approach a specimen examination question on your own.

As you work through the *Practice* sections, you will find:

- **example questions** in the style of examination questions
- **modelled writing**
- a wide range of **texts** exactly like those you will find in the examination papers
- **examiners' advice** on answering questions
- **definitions** of key terms and skills
- **activities** to reinforce the skills being examined
- **prompts** to help you prepare for the real examination
- sample **responses** to questions
- **specimen examination questions**.

Some activities and questions may lend themselves to small- or large-group discussion; others might lead to pieces of writing. Some certainly lend themselves to homework assignments.

The **assessment objectives** and **mark schemes** are set out on pages viii–xii so you know exactly what the examiners are looking for. You are encouraged to check your answers to example and specimen questions against the assessment objectives and mark schemes, and to see how the modelled writing pieces satisfy the assessment objectives.

The book is divided into five chapters, following the organisation of the examination papers:

1 Reading media texts

This chapter looks at Paper 1, Section A, Question 1. Three example media questions are provided, plus a specimen examination question, together with the relevant media texts:

- Practice 1 – example question, with prompts and sample responses
- Practice 2 – example question, with prompts
- Practice 3 – example question, with limited prompts
- Practice 4 – specimen examination question, without prompts.

2 Reading non-fiction texts

Three example questions are provided, plus a specimen examination question, together with the relevant non-fiction texts to help you answer Paper 1, Section A, Question 2:

- Practice 1 – example question, with prompts and sample responses
- Practice 2 – example question, with prompts
- Practice 3 – example question, with prompts and sample responses
- Practice 4 – example question, with prompts
- Practice 5 – specimen examination question, without prompts.

3 Writing to argue, persuade, advise

This chapter is about Paper 1, Section B, Question 3. Strategies for writing are given and practice is provided by the close examination of four modelled pieces of writing, followed by three specimen examination questions:

- Writing to argue, advise
  Practice 1 – modelled writing, with prompts and sample responses
  Practice 2 – modelled writing, with prompts
- Writing to persuade, advise
  Practice 3 – modelled writing, with prompts and sample responses
  Practice 4 – modelled writing, with prompts
- Practice 5–7 – specimen examination questions, without prompts.

4 Reading poetry from different cultures and traditions

Advice is given on how to read poems from different cultures and traditions so you can answer the comparative question: Paper 2, Section A, Question 1. Three example questions and three specimen examination questions are provided:

- Practice 1 – example question, with prompts and sample responses to provide practice in reading a poem
- Practice 2 – example question, with prompts to provide practice in reading a poem
- Practice 3 – example question comparing two poems, with prompts and sample responses
- Practice 4–6 – specimen examination questions, without prompts.

5 Writing to analyse, review, comment

This chapter concentrates on Paper 2, Section B, Question 2. Two pieces of modelled writing, one example question and three specimen examination questions are provided:

- Practice 1 – modelled writing, with prompts and sample responses
- Practice 2 – modelled writing, with prompts
- Practice 3 – example question, with advice and examples
- Practice 4–6 – specimen examination questions, without prompts.

A **glossary** of key terms is provided at the end of the book for quick reference.

Assessment objectives

All examining boards have the same assessment objectives. These are what exam setters use to guide the questions they ask. They will all be tested somewhere in the two papers of the examination.

Reading

i   Read, with insight and engagement, making appropriate references to texts and developing and sustaining interpretations of them;

ii Distinguish between fact and opinion and evaluate how information is presented;

iii Follow an argument, identifying implications and recognising inconsistencies;

iv Select material appropriate to their purpose, collate material from different sources, and make cross-references;

v   Understand and evaluate how writers use linguistic, structural and presentational devices to achieve their effects, and comment on ways language varies and changes.

Writing

i   Communicate clearly and imaginatively, using and adapting forms for different readers and purposes;

ii Organise ideas into sentences, paragraphs and whole texts using a variety of linguistic and structural features

iii Use a range of sentence structures effectively with accurate punctuation and spelling.

Mark schemes

In all specifications for GCSE English, including the AQA Specification B, the marks are split between the questions in the examination as follows:

Paper 1	Section A, Questions 1 and 2: Reading media and non-fiction texts	15%
	Section B, Question 3: Writing to argue, persuade, advise	15%
Paper 2	Section A, Question 1: Reading poetry from different cultures and traditions	15%
	Section B, Question 2: Writing to analyse, review, comment	15%

The remaining marks are allotted to your coursework:

Coursework	Reading	10%
	Writing	10%
	Speaking and listening	20%

The following extracts from mark schemes show what the examiner is looking for in your answer when he or she marks your paper.

Media texts and poetry

Lower mark band

- Show some basic interpretation, insight and understanding of the content of the texts;
- Make some reference to the information and detail presented in the texts;
- Make some appropriate quotation from the texts;
- Show some basic understanding of some of the writers' intentions in the texts;
- Show some limited awareness of how the writers use language, layout and presentation in the texts.

Higher mark band

- Offer a full interpretation, insight and understanding of the content of the texts;
- Make appropriate reference to the information and detail presented in the texts;
- Quote appropriately from the texts;
- Show understanding of some of the writers' intentions in the texts;
- Evaluate how the writers use language, layout and presentation to achieve their intended effect.

Highest mark band

- Offer a full and detailed interpretation, insight and understanding of the content of the texts;
- Make appropriate and comprehensive reference to the information and detail presented in the texts;
- Quote fully and appropriately from the texts;
- Show a full understanding of the writers' intentions in the texts;
- Evaluate and analyse how the writers use language, layout and presentation to achieve their intended effect.

Non-fiction texts

Lower mark band

- Show some basic interpretation, insight and understanding of the content of the non-fiction text;
- Make some reference to the information and detail presented in the text, probably copied or paraphrased;
- Show some basic ability to distinguish fact from opinion;
- Make some appropriate quotation from the texts to support responses.

Higher mark band

- Offer a full interpretation, insight and understanding of the content of the non-fiction text;
- Make appropriate reference to the information and detail presented in the text;
- Show some ability to distinguish fact from opinion;
- Evaluate some aspects of the writing
- Analyse the writer's use of language.
- Offer some quotation in support of responses

Highest mark band

- Offer a full and detailed interpretation, insight and understanding of the content of the non-fiction text;
- Make appropriate and comprehensive reference to the information and detail presented in the text;
- Show ability in distinguishing fact and opinion; evaluate aspects of the writing;

- Give a sustained analysis of the writer's use of language;
- Quote fully and appropriately from the text.

Writing

Argue, persuade, advise

In the mark range for grade C, the examiner will be looking for the effective use of the following skills.

Communication

- Write in a way which shows clarity of thought and communicates with some success;
- Engage the reader with more detailed argument and persuasive ideas;
- Clearly state and sustain the purpose and intention of the writing;
- Write in a formal way, the tone of which is appropriately serious and which may show subtlety, employ e.g. emphasis, assertion, reason;
- Use devices such as the rhetorical question, lists, hyperbole as appropriate;
- Use words effectively including argumentative/persuasive markers, e.g. 'responsibility', 'duty', 'blame', 'conscience', 'how would you like it if …'.

Organisation of ideas

- Employ paragraphs effectively in a whole text;
- Use a variety of structural features, e.g. different paragraph lengths, dialogue, indented sections if appropriate;
- Present well thought out and developed ideas in sentences.

Accuracy

- Write with control of agreement, punctuation and sentence construction;
- Organise writing using sentence demarcation which is mainly accurate;
- Employ a variety of sentence forms;
- Show accuracy in the spelling of words in common use in an increasingly ambitious vocabulary;
- Use standard English appropriately.

Analyse, review, comment

In the mark range for grade C, the examiner will be looking for the effective use of the following skills.

Communication

- Write in a way which shows clarity of thought and communicates with some success;
- Engage the reader with more detailed analysis and carefully considered comments, e.g. make some detailed reference to the issue and the implications of alternative actions;

- Clearly state and sustain the purpose and intention of writing the article, e.g. by stating the writer's comments, alternative courses of action and recommendations;
- Write a formal article, the tone of which is appropriately balanced and which may show subtlety, employ e.g. enquiry, investigation, sifting of evidence;
- Use devices such as the rhetorical question, lists, hyperbole as appropriate;
- Use words effectively including analytical markers, e.g. 'However', 'Alternatively', 'It might be better if …', 'There is a view that …', 'Evidence shows that …'.

Organisation of ideas

- Employ paragraphs effectively in a whole text;
- Use a variety of structural features, e.g. different paragraph lengths, dialogue, indented sections if appropriate;
- Present well thought out and developed ideas in sentences.

Accuracy

- Write with control of agreement, punctuation and sentence construction;
- Organise writing using sentence demarcation which is mainly accurate;
- Employ a variety of sentence forms;
- Show accuracy in the spelling of words in common use in an increasingly ambitious vocabulary;
- Use standard English appropriately.

Paper 1

Paper 1 comprises:

● Section **A**, which examines reading
● Section **B**, which examines writing.

The paper takes 1 hour 40 minutes.

Section A

There are two questions in Section A:

● **Question 1**, which is related to the media material which appears in the pre-release booklet sent to schools. You will study all of the pieces before the exam, but there will be questions on only a selected number.

● **Question 2**, which will ask you to respond to a piece of non-fiction writing, which you will not see before the start of the examination.

Section B

There is one question in Section B:

● **Question 3**, in which you will be asked to produce one piece of writing to argue, persuade, advise on a given topic which will be linked to the themes in the reading material for Section A.

Section A

Section A is a test of reading:

- Question 1 will test your response to media material which you will have studied before the exam.
- Question 2 will test your response to non-fiction material which is 'unseen'.

You are advised to take 1 hour to answer the questions in Section A and they are worth 15 per cent of the final mark.

The questions will relate to the assessment objectives for reading, which are set out on page viii. You will see how these are applied by the person who sets your exam as you work through the Practice sections of this book.

Your examination papers are marked by an examiner who has been trained to look for a number of things in your work. He or she works from a mark scheme. Extracts from a mark scheme for media are set out on pages ix–xi.

1 | Reading media texts

Preparation for this part of the exam takes the form of a pre-release booklet which you study before the exam. On pages 5–8 you will see a number of media stories all taken from newspapers over the New Year period 2001–2002 on the theme of spending, shopping and retailing. This is exactly the sort of material which will be in the pre-release booklet for media. There will be 6–10 media extracts: stories, comment, pictures, headlines, possibly fact-file, letters and cartoons. Both Higher and Foundation tier will study the same material.

Paper 1, Section A, Question 1 of the examination will focus on three or four items from the pre-release booklet – but you won't know which ones until you open the exam paper.

Note: The pre-release booklet also contains the poems for Paper 2, Section A.

The *Practice* sections in this chapter use media material in exactly the same way as in the examination. You are given a lot of help in the first section and this is gradually withdrawn as you progress through the following sections:

- Practice 1, page 4 – the example question looks at media material about spending, shopping and retailing; prompts and sample responses are provided
- Practice 2, page 23 – the example question looks at more media material about spending, shopping and retailing; prompts are provided
- Practice 3, page 35 – the example question looks at media material about winter weather; some limited prompts are provided
- Practice 4, page 43 – the specimen examination question looks at more media material about winter weather; this is exactly like the examination – you are given no help at all.

Practice 1

In this section you are given prompts and possible responses to help you answer the question.

Example question

Read the four articles on pages 5–8. Study the pictures, headlines and captions:

> *We've spent £15 billion*
> *Yes but is it the last hurrah of the boom?*
> *Spending for victory*
> *Cash-happy hordes fill city shops*

and then make a written response to the following questions.

a) What are the main points being made in the article by Alex Brummer?

(Assessment objectives i, ii, iii)

b) Compare the article by Rebecca English and Peter Markham with the one by Simon Peevers in terms of content and the way they are written.

(Assessment objectives i, iv)

c) Find and comment on interesting or vivid use of language in any of the stories.

(Assessment objective v)

d) Explain the purpose and effect of the headlines, sub-headings, captions and pictures presented in the material.

(Assessment objective v)

Assessment objectives

The assessment objectives are given for each part of the question so you can see:

● why the question has been asked
● what the examiners are looking for in your answer.

Go back to page viii to remind yourself of the assessment objectives.

Examiners' advice

You will have studied all of the pre-release pieces *before* the exam. What you must do *in* the exam is to:

● quickly locate the relevant pieces and re-read them – do not refer to any of the other pieces, just those referred to in the question
● think carefully about what you learned and discussed about these pieces
● work through each section of the question in turn

and most important

● answer the question which has been asked – no more and no less.

Sweeping aside all the gloomy predictions, shoppers flock to the sales on a record post-Christmas spree

We've spent £15 billion

Above: *Shoppers pack the streets of Newcastle upon Tyne yesterday*

Left: *Bags of sale bargains at the Bluewater complex near Dartford*

By Rebecca English and Peter Markham

HUNDREDS of thousands of bargain-hunters went sales crazy yesterday, splashing out up to £15billion as Britain revelled in a record-breaking, post-Christmas spending spree.

Some big-name stores estimated that takings were up by as much as 20 per cent on last year.

City analysts had feared that the global economic downturn would result in consumers tightening their belts.

But last night delighted retail chiefs said we are ignoring the doom and gloom prophets and taking advantage of low interest rates.

At Marks & Spencer's flagship store in London's Marble Arch, buyers were scooping up armfuls of half-price cashmere jumpers reduced from £99 to £50.

One member of staff said: 'Some people were grabbing five or six at a time and making for the till points. They could barely have had time to check they had the right size.'

At Selfridges in Oxford Street, the owner of a construction company spent £9,500 on a silver-plated cutlery service reduced from £19,000.

'A wonderful atmosphere'

The unnamed customer and his wife, who live in Berkshire and have their own butler, paid for the 12-piece set with a credit card.

In the Midlands, shoppers began camping out at 12.15am to gain first spot for the 6am opening of the Next sale at the Victoria Centre in Nottingham.

It was a similar picture at Europe's largest shopping centre, Bluewater, near Dartford, Kent.

By the time the doors of the Next branch opened there at 6am, more than 600 bargain-hunters were already queuing round the block. At 7.15am, staff were forced to shut the doors because of the crush inside.

Retail experts said the sudden surge in spending reported just before Christmas seems to have continued – and now looks set to last well into the New Year.

James Bidwell, marketing manager at Selfridges, said shoppers have re-discovered the feelgood factor. …

adapted from *Daily Mail*, 28 December 2001

SHOPPERS are showing a gritty determination to prove the economic soothsayers wrong. The more we predict gloom and doom ahead, the more they spend. It is as if people feel a patriotic duty to shop until they drop so that Britain will remain the one member of the seven richest countries in the world which steers clear of the recession.

Events post-September 11 were meant to make us reluctant to leave our homes. But while shopping malls have emptied in the U.S., we Britons have been spending as if our lives depended on it.

In the run-up to Christmas, it is estimated that a record-breaking £18billion was spent on the High Streets – about twice the national annual output of Kenya. The spending has not stopped there. Having been prepared to pay full prices before Christmas, people now seem to be buying the same goods at stores such as Marks & Spencer at prices 40 per cent cheaper.

This extra £15billion post-Christmas spending is expected to bring the total holiday shopping bill up to £33billion.

So what are the factors driving this spending psychosis?

Nearly a decade of non-stop expansion of the economy has inured us to bad news. A generation has come of age in a period of solidly rising house prices, nearly full employment and a bubbling stock market.

Graduates get jobs straight from university and even the dispossessed have been enriched by Gordon Brown's generosity through the 'New Deal' for unemployed youth.

In addition, the working families tax credit has boosted the minimum income of the lowest paid in society.

It has proved nearly impossible to

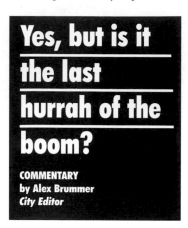

Yes, but is it the last hurrah of the boom?

COMMENTARY
by Alex Brummer
City Editor

shift expectations that the good times will keep rolling. In 1997–98, as emerging market nations from Thailand to Russia crashed like ninepins, it looked for a brief few months as if Britain would follow suit.

Even the Government was shaken and hurried to revise growth prospects downwards. But with characteristic defiance, British consumers saw the meltdown as an opportunity to buy goods from the deflating Far East. Another reason is that lending has become so easy. Even those with no income of their own, like my 19-year-old son in his gap year between school and university, are bombarded with offers of credit cards with near zero interest rates. …

So, as we look ahead, consumers are again being asked to keep Britain moving in the face of world crisis. Except this time the task looks much harder than during the last consumer boom. It is not just a few Asian economies in trouble, but much of the industrialised world. …

The current consumer boom suggests people refuse to be shaken by events abroad. They are also being supported by a government which after years of restraint is pouring money into the public services.

What is not clear is if all this will be enough to keep danger at bay. Personal financial security, on which strong spending is built, could come undone in the coming months.

House prices, one of the underpinnings of prosperity, will rise more slowly next year and the Halifax forecast an increase of five per cent compared with 11 per cent last year.

Unemployment, which remained low through most of the last year, began to creep up in October and November. This could prove a turning point.

What is truly disquieting is that for many borrowers, including those out with their credit cards this week, the reckoning could be approaching.

A combination of falling house prices, rising unemployment and a weak stock market will increase insecurity and make people less able to service their debts.

So far, levels of arrears among people with mortgages, credit card bills and bank loans remain relatively modest by historical standards. Low interest rates allow people to meet their obligations.

But with debts at record levels and confidence subsiding, it is possible the present paroxysm of spending is the last hurrah of the boom.

adapted from *The Mail on Sunday*, 30 December 2001

Spending for victory

Shoppers put on a dazzling display over the Christmas period of what the great economist John Maynard Keynes prescribed as the antidote to the Great Depression of the 1930s – "animal spirit". Ignoring the gloomsters, buyers surged into department stores and shopping malls with one recession-defying aim in mind: spend, spend, spend. The story was the same across the country. Retail sales surged by 10% and more, and motorway queues to the biggest shopping centres became so long that people had to put their credit cards on hold for 45 minutes before they could unleash them.

The psychology of it is obvious enough. We have got over the shock of September 11, horrific though it was, and decided to get on with our lives. Job prospects don't look so good in the new year, but Keynes would applaud the 220,000 people who thronged Manchester's Trafford Centre shops in two hectic days, and millions more like them.

Yesterday's news from America told the same story of renewed consumer confidence. Home sales and purchases of big-ticket items like cars, home appliances and electronic equipment surged so strongly that economists are talking about an end to the US recession this coming year. Low interest rates have undoubtedly fuelled the rise in retail sales, but there is more to it than that. Wall Street analysts say "we're not out of the woods yet", but there is no doubting that public's longing to be.

Even the remote but undeniable prospect of sitting next to a crank on a plane failed to deter American travellers from flying in large numbers again over the holiday. More than 2m Americans took to the skies on Boxing Day and Thursday, filling 85% of available seats. Will consumers keep their nerve on this side of the pond? The omens are good. Inflation is low and likely to stay that way. The stock market has held up better than the jeremiahs predicted and most pundits expect an upturn. …

adapted from *Sunday Times*, 30 December 2001

First day of the sales 'breaks all records'

CASH-HAPPY HORDES FILL CITY SHOPS

by SIMON PEEVERS

WITH the frenzy of the first day of the sales over, retailers in Bristol are looking forward to a bumper January.

John Hirst manager at Broadmead, said the booming economy has given shoppers the confidence to come out in droves and that the events of September 11 had helped to boost sales.

He said: "I think this year people have decided to stay at home (rather than go on foreign holidays), which has benefited us because people have more money to spend at this time of year.

"It was at fever pitch yesterday, as it always is on the first day, and that meant it was great trading for businesses in Broadmead.

"But there are three reasons why sales are good. It is partly to do with the economy, which is in good shape.

"It's to do with the confidence people feel, having money in their pockets.

"And it has a lot to do with Bristol being a major destination.

"Many more people are coming to Bristol and the South West now for holidays, which means they come and shop here. The region as a whole is doing very well."

Sue Boor, marketing manager at the Mall, Cribbs Causeway, said that people were keen to get out of the house and spend money after Christmas. She said: "Shopping is a leisure activity and people want to go to the sales for a day out.

"A lot of people have presents they want to change and gift cheques they want to spend.

"People do have more money at the moment and the low interest rates are giving people the confidence to spend.

"We expect trade to be steady although it will probably be much quieter when the schools open again."

The traffic chaos in Bristol is set to continue today as people head for sales. A traffic police spokesman said: "We expect it to be as bad today as it was on Thursday. A lot of people are still off work and will be going shopping.

"Our advice is to stagger journeys; to go early or late. But if people do get caught in traffic they need to take it easy.

"We had a lot of angry people calling our line telling us to switch off traffic lights, but that

Taking a breather: Two well-laden bargain-hunters have a rest and decide on their next target

is nothing to do with us, that is the city council's responsibility."

The sales are set to continue for the next two weeks.

Bristol Evening Post, 28 December 2001

Approaches to part (a) of the example question

This section will teach you about:

- understanding the content of the article with insight and engagement
- developing and sustaining interpretation of the article
- distinguishing between fact and opinion
- following an argument, identifying implications.

Before you answer part (a) of the example question, check that you understand the following definitions and try the activities. They will help you to understand the assessment objectives.

Definitions

'understanding the content of the article with *insight* and *engagement*'

This really means that you should focus carefully on the text so that you understand it.

- To have **insight** means to understand what it really means.
- To **engage** means to connect with.

Activity 1.1

Focus on *engagement*.

Read the first few paragraphs from the article by Alex Brummer. What is it about this article which *connects with* people who might read it?

You should think about:

- who the people involved are – are they like anybody you know?
- what these people have been doing
- what is interesting about some of the figures and examples he quotes.

Now you have *engaged with* the article.

Activity 1.2

Focus on *insight*.

The article is obviously about people spending money. But what other point is being made?

Think about:

- the reasons he gives for the spending boom
- what happened 'from Thailand to Russia'
- what might happen in Britain.

Now you are reading with *insight*.

Definitions

'*developing* and *sustaining* interpretation of the article'

This means that you need to show that you understand what the writer is getting at. You need to begin your interpretation (*develop it*) and make sure it fully answers the question (that it is *sustained*).

- To **develop** means *to begin, commence.*
- To **sustain** means *to keep going.*

Activity 1.3

As we saw above, the article is obviously about spending money.
But what more is the writer saying?

Think about:

- why he uses the word 'meltdown'
- which words in the last three paragraphs are similar in meaning to 'crash' and 'meltdown'.

Do you think the writer stays on the same topic throughout?

Definitions

'distinguishing between *fact* and *opinion*'

- A **fact** is something which is real, which actually happened, which is true. Facts can be shown or demonstrated. For example, 'It is a fact that Britain has a railway system.'
- An **opinion** is a belief, a feeling, an idea, an impression, a point of view. Opinions may be strongly held and they may be based on good reasons; but they are not facts. For example, 'In my opinion, Britain's railway system is very good!'

Activity 1.4

Focus on *fact and opinion*.

1 Write down a fact about:

   a) aeroplanes
   b) school dinners
   c) examinations
   d) football.

2 Write down an opinion about each of these.

Activity 1.5

Focus on *fact and opinion*.

Which of these statements from Alex Brummer's article is a fact and which is an opinion?

1   'This extra £15 billion post Christmas spending is expected to bring the total holiday shopping bill up to £33 billion.'
2   'Even the government was shaken and hurried to revise growth prospects downwards.'
3   'The current consumer boom suggests that people refuse to be shaken by events abroad.'
4   'House prices will rise more slowly next year.'
5   'It is possible that the present paroxysm of spending is the last hurrah of the boom.'

Definitions

'follow an *argument, identifying implications*'

- An **argument** means a point of view or several points of view.
- **Implication** means what else does the writer think will happen; what are the side effects?
- **Identifying** means reading the text carefully and finding the side effects.

Activity 1.6

Focus on *implication*.

In the last few paragraphs Brummer says that house prices will rise more slowly next year and unemployment will creep up. In the third to last paragraph he states two implications of this. What are they?

Now answer part (a) of the example question:

a)   What are the main points being made in the article by Alex Brummer?

(Assessment objectives i, ii, iii)

Examiners' advice

- The responses are presented here as notes, but you should write your answer as continuous prose. These notes would easily convert into two paragraphs.
- The responses include the main points of Brummer's article and would at least satisfy a mark in the higher mark band. Go back to page ix to remind yourself of the mark scheme.

- Your response, like the one below, should be a combination of your own words, some words paraphrased from the text and some quotations.
- You need to show that you can select relevant points from the text to answer the question. This will help you to gain marks.

PROMPTS

▶ Write down the main point in your own words – the clue is in the title/headline.

▶ Mention the audience – the writer's intended readers. Who is he 'talking' to?

▶ What is the purpose of the article?

▶ Write down a general overview of the article; in this case there are two distinct parts to it.

▶ Write down the topic sentence from each paragraph.

▶ Show you understand that some of Brummer's points are facts and some are opinions.

▶ Write down some key phrases as quotations as you go through.

Combine the points above into sentences.

Possible responses

Here are some possible responses to the prompts above. Check them against what you found.

- Alex Brummer warns that the current confident spending spree may turn to personal debt and insecurity in the near future.
- Brummer's audience is the people who have been spending lots of money in the shops. His purpose is to make them stop a moment and think.
- As the 'City Editor' he calls himself an 'economic soothsayer' who predicted 'doom and gloom' ahead for shops and shopping, but so far shoppers are proving him wrong by spending an estimated £18 billion in the run-up to Christmas. They are likely to spend about the same after Christmas.
- He cites a number of reasons for this. For example, we have become so used to hearing 'bad news' that we now ignore it in the context of 'rising house prices, full employment and a bubbling stock market'.
- Other factors which make us feel good about the present include the fact that poorer families and individuals are better off through the 'New Deal' or 'tax credits'. Lending has also become easier for all.

- Events such as terrorism abroad have not shaken the 'current consumer boom'.

But

- Brummer warns that these factors could become less secure in the future; house prices will rise more slowly, unemployment 'began to creep up' in the autumn, the stock market could weaken and although interest rates remain low, these factors 'will increase insecurity and make people less able to service their debts'.
- Some of the points Brummer makes are obviously facts, such as the amount of money which has passed through the tills, factors concerned with the economy, research statistics about credit and lending. But there is also opinion and speculation about, for example, what might happen in the future; whether this is the 'last hurrah' or not.
- Therefore we could be seeing the 'last hurrah of the boom'; in the near future problems of debt and financial insecurity will beset us.

continued

continued

More to think about

There are other points of interest or detail which might be included. See if you can locate them, but you need to paraphrase them (explain them in your own words) and quote appropriately. For example:

- what is an economic soothsayer?
- people feel a 'patriotic duty to shop'

- the expectation that the good times will continue is difficult to change
- the relevance of the events of 11 September
- more detail on personal financial security or insecurity
- what does 'last hurrah' actually mean?

Now incorporate these points into your answer.

Approaches to part (b) of the example question

This section will teach you about:

- collating and selecting material from different sources
- making cross-references.

Before you answer part (b) of the example question, check that you understand the following definitions and try the activities. They will help you to understand the assessment objectives.

Definitions

'collating and selecting material from different sources making cross-references'

- To **collate** means to put texts next to each other and compare them.
- To **select material** means to choose appropriate information or quotations from the articles to use in your answer.
- **Different sources** means the two articles being compared.
- To **make cross-references** means to see what is similar or different between the two texts.

Activity 1.7

Focus on *collating*.

The articles by Peevers and by English and Markham mention places where people shop.

1   Write a list of the shopping places mentioned in each article.
2   What was similar about the behaviour of shoppers in some of the places?
3   What does **collating** this information tell you about the general pattern of shopping in the country?

Activity 1.8
Focus on *collating*.

1   At the end of the Peevers article some advice is given. Does the English/Markham story offer advice?
2   What is similar about the two pictures?
3   What did you notice about the amount of direct quotation used when you collated the two articles?

Now answer part (b) of the example question:

b)   Compare the article by Rebecca English and Peter Markham with the one by Simon Peevers in terms of content and the way they are written.

Examiners' advice

- You need to show that you understand the texts and that you have engaged with them.
- You need to be very obviously *comparing* the two texts.

PROMPTS

▶   Write down what the English/ Markham story is about in your own words. Include a couple of brief quotes to tie your remarks to the text.
▶   Write down what the Peevers story is about in your own words. Include some quotations to support what you write.

▶   Note any similarities and differences in content, material, place, time, events reported between the two articles.
▶   Remember: you are only being asked about the text, not about the pictures, headlines, etc.
▶   Remember to compare, collate and make cross-references between the articles.

Possible responses

Here are some possible responses to the prompts above. Check them against what you found.

- The English/Markham story is about the fact that up to £15 billion has been spent in a post-Christmas 'spending spree'. It says that, despite the fears of city analysts whose predictions were being ignored, shops like Marks and Spencer were reporting business up 'by as much as 20 per cent on last year'. Customers seemed to be buying 'armfuls of half-price cashmere jumpers' regardless of price or size. The article is based in Oxford Street, London, and gives examples of people spending large amounts of money such as the man who bought a £9,500 silver-plated cutlery service, saving himself nearly £10,000.
- Simon Peever's story is set in Bristol where, like in London, retailers are 'looking forward to a bumper January'. The story suggests reasons why sales are so high:

continued

continued

John Hirst, a shop manager says this is because the economy is in good shape, people feel confident with money in their pockets and Bristol is a 'major destination' for shoppers. Another person interviewed suggested that people saw the sales as a way to get out of the house after Christmas. She also agreed that people had the confidence to spend; she said that trade was likely to be steady but added that it 'will probably be much quieter when the schools open again'.

● Both articles are about the post-Christmas sales, the boom in business, the confidence of the shoppers, the volume of sales. Both are centered in major shopping areas, Broadmead and the Mall in Bristol and Oxford Street in London. Both make some reference to economic conditions.

● Peevers' article is longer and fuller — there are direct interviews and quotations from two people. There is some detail offered about the reasons for shoppers' behaviour.

● English and Markham concentrate on examples of what some shoppers bought, volume and price, whereas Peevers concentrates on the opinions and observations of two retailers.

Use the material above to write a two-paragraph response to the question.

More to think about
There might be further points to consider:

● the 'pace' or sense of excitement in the stories
● the relevance of recent global factors common to each article
● more detail on the different levels of analysis in the two pieces
● the use of direct quotation in both articles — the Peevers piece is mostly direct quotation, what about the other piece?
● whether you feel more included in one piece or the other because of the writer's style.

Add these ideas to your answer.

Approaches to part (c) of the example question

This section will teach you about:

● how the writers use language for effect
● the need to keep audience in mind
● how language is used effectively in different articles.

Before you answer part (c) of the example question, check that you understand the following definitions and try the activities. They will help you to understand the assessment objectives.

Definitions
'how the writers use *language* for *effect*'

● **Language** is the way we express ourselves through words.
● **Effective language** is the way we make the most of those words.

Activity 1.9

Focus on *effective language*.

Look at the article 'Cash-happy hordes...'

1 Think about the writer's use of the word 'hordes'.

    a) What does it mean?
    b) Why is it appropriate?

2 Find other interesting words used in the first two paragraphs.
3 In 'Spending for victory' the writer has written, 'dazzling display'. What kind of writing device is this?
4 Make up some more words which mean the same as 'gloomsters'.

Activity 1.10

Focus on *effective language*.

1 Look up and write down the definitions of:

    a) cliché
    b) aphorism
    c) rhetorical question
    d) hyperbole.

2 Write two examples of each.
3 Swap your ideas with a partner.

Activity 1.11

Focus on *effective language*.

The use of vivid and interesting nouns, adjectives, verbs and adverbs are the most direct way to write effective language.

1 Write down definitions of these parts of speech:

    a) noun
    b) adjective
    c) verb
    d) adverb.

2 Look at a paragraph from any of the four articles in this Practice section and write an analysis of the writers' use of:

    a) nouns and adjectives
    b) verbs and adverbs.

There are some good ones in 'Spending for victory'.

Definition

'The need to keep *audience* in mind'

The **audience** for a piece of writing is the person or people who the writer intends will read it. For example, in the articles in this *Practice* section, there are a number of audiences. All of the pieces are about the amount of money spent shopping. So:

- Shoppers are the audience.
- People who spend and don't save are another audience.
- Everybody who buys the *Daily Mail* or *Bristol Evening Post* is the audience.
- The journalist's editor is an audience.
- Students studying media pieces are a further audience.

Activity 1.12

Focus on *audience*.

Think about anything you have recently written; not just in school but anywhere, for example, text messages, a chat room, shopping list, etc.

Who was your audience in each case?

Now answer part (c) of the example question:

c) Find and comment on interesting or vivid use of language in any of the stories.

Examiners' advice

- You know that there is a further question on headlines and pictures following this, so *restrict your response here to the body of the texts*.
- Look carefully at the texts – professional writers, and particularly journalists, use a lot of **linguistic devices**.
- It is helpful if you have some knowledge of the target audiences for different UK newspapers.
- Remember that the word 'media' is the plural of the word 'medium' which is 'a means of communicating between two extremes' – your job here is to examine the way that has been done.
- Quote examples from the text – one word or short phrase examples are the best.
- The responses suggested here would be worth a mark in the higher mark band. Go back to page ix to remind yourself of the mark scheme.

Definition

Linguistic features/devices These include:

- **rhetorical questions**, see the definition on page 109, but these should not be overdone
- **lists** for emphasis and to reinforce an idea
- **command**, because it colours the tone of the writing effectively.
- **ironic statements**
- **satire** and **humour**.

Quoting from experts, officials, spokespersons and referring to scientific or other 'authorities' is also a linguistic device. Sometimes they are entirely made up, but still effective.

PROMPTS

▶ Look for the use of cliché, aphorism and other predictable catch phrases. Note them down.

▶ Look for any rhetorical devices (devices which help to persuade a reader, for example, rhetorical questions, dramatic or exaggerated language) and make a note of them.

▶ Find and write down interesting or vivid verbs, adjectives and adverbs as single words or phrases.

▶ Make reference to the writer's sense of audience and the purpose of his or her writing.

▶ Explain or analyse how and why the writer has chosen the language he or she has used.

▶ There are lots of examples in Alex Brummer's article and in 'Spending for victory'.

Possible responses

Here are some examples of what you might find from Alex Brummer's article. There are lots of examples in the other stories too. Check them against what you found.

- In his first paragraph Brummer uses a number of clichés: 'gritty determination', 'gloom and doom', 'shop until they drop', 'steers clear'. These are deliberately used; they are colourful, and commonly used, and their familiarity will entice the reader into a quite long article. Some readers might assume a deliberate sense of humour on the part of the journalist.
- 'Patriotic duty' and 'the one member of the seven richest countries in the world' are phrases intended to appeal to a particular audience – *Daily Mail* readers might be supposed to be patriotic on the whole.
- 'Inured', which means 'become used to', is not a common word; the writer is complimenting the intelligence of his readership by using it. Posing the question, 'So what are the factors …?' is a rhetorical question which draws the reader into the article and opens up the way for the writer to express his views.
- Brummer next uses lists to enumerate his views and introduces the world view, '… nations from Thailand to Russia crashed like ninepins'. This sentence combines a sense of worldly authority and knowledge with a disarming cliché. The first section of his article is concluded with a personal touch, 'like my 19 year old son in his gap year'; the effect of this is to ensure empathy with thousands of his readers and indirectly with thousands more (i.e. he is just like all his readers – he identifies with them).
- The use of language changes in the latter part of the article. His **tone** changes to

continued

continued

one of warning and concern. Words such as 'danger', 'come undone', 'underpinnings of prosperity', 'truly disquieting', 'the reckoning', 'falling', 'weak', 'debts' pepper the article with a sense of foreboding to hold the reader to the end. The very effective word 'paroxysm' is left until the last suggesting, as it does, a fit preceding death.

● The writer is clearly aware of his audience, their mood, their capacity for difficult

ideas and language. The article makes a specific point in an entertaining way with a specific readership in mind.

Write your answer in continuous prose.

More to think about
Following the example above, and looking for similar things, now read 'We've spent £15 billion' and, particularly, 'Spending for victory'. Write your analysis of these two articles in continuous prose.

Definition

The **tone** of a piece of writing is its overall mood — it tells us of a writer's attitude towards his or her subject. Thinking about the tone is a good starting point. What is the feel of the piece? Is it serious? Light-hearted? Angry? Sad?

Approaches to part (d) of the example question

This section will teach you about:

● how the writers have used presentational devices
● the importance of pictures
● how pictures relate to headlines and stories.

Before you answer part (d) of the example question, check that you understand the following definition and try the activities. They will help you to understand the assessment objectives.

Definition

'how the writers have used *presentational devices*'

Presentational devices are the different ways the material is presented visually — the way it looks, the positioning of the text and illustrations. The text is all of the writing, and the illustrations include photographs, cartoons, graphs, tables and charts. The editor arranges them in such a way as to make them most interesting and engaging to the reader.

Activity 1.13

Focus on *presentational devices*.

Look at the article by Simon Peevers. Let your eyes roam over the whole piece. You can see that there are six separate blocks or sections presented to you. The first two are:

- the headline, 'Cash-happy hordes fill city shops' in heavy block capital letters to stand out
- the grey block which says, 'by Simon Peevers'.

Find and describe the other four.

Activity 1.14

Focus on *presentational devices*.

Make up a presentation block for a story of your own. You might take it from something you have read, for example 'The Murder of King Duncan from *Macbeth*'.

Design the presentation of the story. You will need:

- the main text
- some paragraph headers
- a headline
- a sub-headline
- two pictures
- two captions
- the reporter's name.

Now answer part (d) of the example question:

d) Explain the purpose and effect of the headlines, sub-headings, captions and pictures presented in the material.

Examiners' advice

- There is much to write about in the analysis of headlines, pictures and the other presentational devices. Look at the whole story as presented – everything on the page or inside the margin.
- Look for the connections and relationships between the parts.
- Then find similarities and contrasts between the articles you are studying.
- Remember: you are the audience. The writer, photographer and editor have you in mind when the story is put together, so refer to this in your comments.

PROMPTS

▶ Look at all of the headlines first and see which stand out and ask yourself why; it might be size of letters, the words used, the position on the page, or all three.

▶ Do the same thing with the pictures.

▶ Remember that the super-headings or abstract (the writing above the headline), the sub-headings (the headings below the main headline or between paragraphs) and the

continued

PROMPTS *continued*

- photograph captions are also important.
- Do not be afraid to make some obvious statements but try to find interesting or subtle meanings or connections between the headlines, stories and pictures.
- Where there are combinations of presentational devices, deal with them altogether so that you can show the links and connections between them.

Possible responses

Here are some possible responses to the prompts above. Check them against what you found.

'We've spent £15 billion'

- This headline is written in very large bold font, lower case and spans the whole width of the page. The use of 'We' involves the reader immediately and includes him or her in the article. This will encourage the readers' interest. The '£15 billion' is factual, as the article goes on to explain, but it is a huge sum of money, and including it in the headline will also interest and involve readers.

- The super-headline or abstract links directly to the headline, though it probably wouldn't be read first. 'Sweeping aside' is a clichéd **metaphor**, but an effective one with immediate meaning. 'Flock' is also a cliché, but the description is of ordinary, mass activity rather than anything special so the words are deliberate and effective. Clichés are appropriate because the writer wants to communicate directly and immediately with the reader. Go back to Activity 1.10 to remind yourself about clichés.

- There are two pictures on the page. Each is large and together they occupy about half of the page. The caption tells us that in one 'shoppers pack the streets', which looks like a shopping precinct, in Newcastle upon Tyne, a place not referred to in the accompanying story. The super-imposed picture is also explained in the caption; Bluewater in Kent is referred to. The woman is happy and confident, words which are reflected in the paragraph heading, 'A wonderful atmosphere', which is intended to reinforce the tone of the story. She is laden with sales shopping bags which project out of the picture towards the reader. Next is a smart store and the ordinariness of the woman makes the point that in the sales we can all afford to shop at Next. The presentation has life, pace, excitement, even a sense of adventure – all of which the editor has deliberately created to involve the reader.

'Yes, but is it the last hurrah of the boom?'

- The headline is also large font, lower case but with white letters on a black background which also includes 'Commentary' in block letters indicating that this is an article not a report.

- The writer's name is accompanied by his title 'City Editor'.

- The headline, which is a topic sentence from the text, is also underlined which lends importance to it. The headline is a direct link from the 'We've spent …' one. In fact, it is a response or reply to it; it is intended to balance the confident euphoria described above with a warning. The purpose is to stop the reader in his or her excitement and make them think, then read the article. 'Yes, but' are the words which will do this.

'Cash-happy hordes fill city shops'

- The headline is a large font, upper-case, black blocked capitals headline with the writer's name underneath.

continued on page 22

continued from page 21

- 'Cash-happy' summarises in a hyphenated adjective one of the points in the story – that there is plenty of money being spent in Bristol's stores.
- 'Hordes' is an interesting word; it suggests that massed shoppers 'fighting' for bargains are threatening or dangerous. The word lends a different tone to the article, in contrast to the previous sense of happiness and euphoria. It reflects the phrase 'fever-pitch' which is used in the story and the word 'target' used in the caption to the picture.
- The editor seems to favour hyphenated words; two more feature in the caption, 'well-laden' and 'bargain-hunters', as well as the use of **alliteration** in 'happy hordes'.

- The purpose of the headline here seems to be to set a quite different tone to the one established in 'We've spent …'; a tone reflected in the less exuberant story.

More to think about
- Contrast the picture in 'Cash-happy hordes' with those in 'We've spent …'.
- Could there be a pun indicated between 'hordes' and 'hoards'?
- How might 'Spending for victory' be like 'digging for victory'? And what victory anyway?
- Do you think any of these presentations are particularly successful? Why?

Now write your answer in continuous prose.

Definitions
- **Metaphor** is when a writer writes about something as if it is something else so you see it in a new way.
- **Alliteration** is the deliberate repetition of a consonant sound for effect, usually the first letter, for example, *the slippery snake slid stealthily sideways*.

Check your answer

1   When you have completed your answer to the example question:
   a) check that you have satisfied all the assessment objectives for reading (see page viii)
   b) look at the mark scheme for reading media texts on page ix – which mark band do you think your answer is in? Explain why.
2   If your teacher marks your answer, consider his or her comments and how your mark fits in the mark scheme. Which mark band is your answer in? Can you see why?
3   Consider what you could try to do to move into a higher mark band.

Practice 2

In *Practice 1*, you looked at four media items and an example question. You were shown how to approach the question and provided with answers. In *Practice 2*, you will study four more pieces of media text on the same theme and another example question. You will be given prompts for responding to the question, but this time, there are no answers – you will have to write them yourself.

Example question

Read the four articles on pages 24–7 and study the pictures, headlines and captions:

> *Darkness at heart of consumer spending spree*
> *In the Retail Temple, worshipping frantically*
> *Shopping: it's a guy thing*
> *The first casualty of shopping is the truth*

and then make a written response to the following questions.

a) What are the main points being made in the article 'Shopping: it's a guy thing'?
(Assessment objectives i, ii, iii)

b) Compare the leading article from *The Scotsman* and the article by Robert Hardman in terms of their content and style.
(Assessment objectives i, iv)

c) Find and comment on interesting or vivid use of language in any of the stories.
(Assessment objective v)

d) Explain the purpose and effect of the headlines, sub-headings, captions and pictures presented in the material.
(Assessment objective v)

Assessment objectives

The assessment objectives are given for each part of the question so you can see:

- why the question has been asked
- what the examiners are looking for in your answer.

Go back to page viii to remind yourself of the assessment objectives.

Approaches to part (a) of the example question

This section will teach you about:

- understanding, insight of and engagement with the text
- the importance of understanding the audience at whom the article is aimed
- the difference between fact and opinion in the article.

Darkness at the heart of consumer spending spree

Against the most sombre international background for a decade, Britain is cruising into 2002 with consumer spending roaring ahead at its fastest pace in thirteen years. Not only are sales in the high street up by 7% on a year ago, but there is also a surge in winter holiday bookings. Fear of travel terrorism has given way to the hunger for holidays in the sun.

It would be comforting to take this spending surge at face value – a celebration of resilient economic performance and an expression of confidence in the future. But it is open to an alternative, altogether darker explanation. This is that we have so little confidence in the future, that the world has become an altogether more insecure and uncertain place, that we opt to spend heavily now out of a sense that the future is going to be much, much worse.

It is not that the public finds little incentive to save in an era verging on deflation. It is that the terrorist attacks of 11 September have changed the mood, not just in the United States, but around the world, and with it a change in all previous assumptions about risk and certainty. Whether this spending boom is thus an orthodox expression of consumer confidence, or a psychological portent of something more profound will be the big issue of 2002. But, for the moment, it does seem as if our confidence extends little further than today's bargain sale.

We are happy to splurge out on 'big ticket' items in the stores and on foreign holidays in winter, while personal pension provision is running woefully short of that required to assure a decent life in old age. Indeed, the savings ratio, far from rising as it classically does in periods of economic downturn, has continued to fall. It is now down to just 5% of household income, or less than half the level of the early and mid 1990s.

This collapse in savings is storing up big trouble. It puts a question over not just the repayment of personal debt, now being taken on at an alarming rate, but also the ability of an aging population to look after itself in retirement.

adapted from *The Scotsman*, 28 December 2001

In the Retail Temple, worshipping frantically

HOW I SEE IT
by
Robert Hardman

IF RECESSION is stalking these halls and shop floors, it is proving as elusive as Bin Laden.

It is not just a busy day at Lakeside Shopping Centre, Thurrock – reputedly the largest in Europe. Day one of the sales season is proving to be the busiest day in the 11-year history of Essex's mighty temple to the god of retail.

By closing time, 160,000 people were expected to have passed through the doors.

Whichever way you try to quantify that figure – call it two FA Cup final crowds, one-and-a-half times the British Army, more than half the people in Iceland – it is a lot of people.

Despite a Christmas which saw spending go through the roof, most of this gawping, shuffling peoplescape are here to spend even more. Each will have spent an average of £125 by the end of the day.

'We are 25 per cent up on last year which was a record year and that was 30 per cent up on the year before,' says David Shone, founder of independent jewellers Emson-Haig.

His stocks of a certain £1,050 Gucci watch were dancing out of the shops before Christmas and he has already sold out of them. It was a great Christmas for diamonds too. Over at Next, it is bedlam. Its sale started at 6am, four hours before the rest of the centre. Even so, there were 2,500 cars here at 5am just to be first inside for half-price clothes.

Nine hours later, it is still heaving with sharp-elbowed Essex girls. To stand still in the gangway is to cause a pile-up.

Outside, Matthew Peterson-Bearce, 30, is enjoying a brief respite from a morning of hand-to-hand combat with the debit card.

He has been buying a DVD drive and CDs. 'Last Christmas, I spent £3,000 on presents. This year, it's closer to £7,500, though that did include an engagement trip to New York,' he says.

He works in the IT department of a London bank and takes a stoical view of the economy: 'You can't take it with you when you go.' Despite statistics showing credit card debt has reached a peak of 107 per cent of disposable income for the average household, few of today's Lakeside shoppers are spending what they haven't got. And most of those I talk to exude a quiet contentment about the state of the economy. ...

I head for Lakeside's management offices in search of illumination.

There, however, marketing manager Heather Hudson-Oldnall tells me: 'Sales in the first three quarters of the year were up by eight per cent on the previous year and the last two months have been up 12 per cent with something like a six to ten per cent rise in Christmas numbers.'

In other words, not only have more people been coming, they have been spending more per head too. And the spending goes on and on.

Fleeing the piped music and mayhem for the relative calm of an M25 traffic jam, I am none the wiser as to how or why we have all this money. The question now, surely, is this: how much longer can it all go on?

adapted from *The Mail on Sunday*, 30 December 2001

FOCUS

As tills ring with record takings, men are out in force at the sales. Gone are the days when they had to be dragged round the shops. **Margarette Driscoll** and **Jane Mulkerrins** report on the emergence of men who love to buy

SHOPPING
IT'S A GUY THING

> **'** Men are adopting more female values. It is a lot more acceptable for men to be interested in design these days **'**

There was something odd afoot at the sales last week – and not just the queues that began at 3am for an early-morning stampede into Next.

Among the crowds that thronged the pavements of Oxford Street in London and blocked the car park at Bluewater in Kent and the MetroCentre on Tyneside were hundreds of thousands of men – not dragged along on pain of death, but there voluntarily.

Men, who would traditionally work off their Christmas indulgence at the footie or beside a racecourse, are becoming Britain's most conspicuous consumers.

It may seem unbelievable to most women, but the average man secretly enjoys shopping. He shops for clothes slightly more often than his female counterpart – and high street stores, waking up to his spending power, are doing everything from providing newspapers to sports coverage to tempt him in.

Men were there at the ready as the doors opened for the sales. At Harvey Nichols in Knightsbridge, London, male shoppers fought for bargains "shoulder to shoulder" in a heaving men's section; at Selfridges, also in London, where menswear sales have doubled in the past five years, David Pauy, 27, was out to buy luxury goods, clothes and electrical items and was not afraid to admit that he liked shopping.

"It's my only vice," he said. "I don't smoke, I don't drink very much and I like to spend money. I go shopping whenever I can."

His wife Jane confirmed his addiction. "He goes shopping more than me," she said.

The key difference between the sexes is that one "goes shopping" and the other "does the shopping". Most men are still hopeless at the latter (although, intriguingly, 39% of men in the Midlands claim to do the weekly shop). The big change in male spending habits has come about in "hobby shopping" – Saturday or Sunday afternoons spent at the shops, browsing.

Advertisers know that men are spending more than ever on clothes. Spending on advertisements for fashionable sports and leisurewear has risen from £9m to £25.9m in the past five years. Over the same period, advertising on men's fashion has risen from £6.9m to £13.3m.

The British menswear market is growing steadily. Last year it reached £6.5 billion and is predicted to grow by 9.9% – more quickly than the women's market – over the next five years. British men spent an average of £250 on clothes last year, compared with a paltry £73 spent by French men.

The Sunday Times, 30 December 2001

The lies we tell when hubby spots yet another bag of 'absolutely vital bargains'

FLIC EVERETT

The first casualty of shopping is the truth

It's that time of year again. The post-Christmas sales when the nation, particularly the female half, takes to the High Street in search of bargains. It is also the time when we women tax our ingenuity to the utmost in finding ways of keeping our expensive (but, of course, essential) purchases from our partners.

For some reason, despite having our own bank accounts, earning our own money and taking no prisoners when it comes to relationship rights, the one area that seemingly plunges us straight back to Upstairs-Downstairs,

> **'A girl I know arrives home laden with shiny designer boutique bags and claims everything was 75 per cent off'**

Master Of The House mode is clothes shopping.

A new survey by an Internet bank has discovered that more than 25 per cent of women conceal their purchases. It also reveals that, when those purchases are wisps of clothing costing more than lagging the loft and retiling the bathroom put together, 90 per cent turn into blushing, stammering fibbers, clutching the Harvey Nichols carri-

ers behind them as they edge from the room backwards.

Of course, this method of shopping relies on the unobservant nature of men and, given that most wouldn't know Halston from Hennes, or even Ozbek from Oxfam for that matter, it's perfectly easy for a woman to claim her new cashmere is just a jumper her friend "lent" her when she was cold or to insist she's had that high-fashion skirt for months with a forceful: "I just haven't bothered wearing it much." Sadly, my husband had been exposed to so many of my immense wardrobe's permutations on Saturday nights, as I agonise between 15 different outfits and interrupt his shaving routine for

advice, that he can spot a new addition with more accuracy than a leopard pinpointing the lame antelope in the herd.

I have a friend who claims not to have bought anything new for five years, despite engaging in a weekly campaign of bag concealment (she folds them up very small and stuffs the into the bottom of the bin). Another girl I know arrives home laden with shiny, full-price bags from designer boutiques and claims that everything was 75 per cent off – she might get away with this ruse were it not for the fact that she tries it two weeks before Christmas when sales are no more than a twinkle in shoppers' eyes.

But there's no point in even trying to deceive

my husband like this. He is far too well versed in current fashion, can accurately fix an astronomic price to within £5 and not only recognises designer clothes but can identify the designers without even looking at the label.

So when, in a moment of pure adrenaline-fuelled insanity which I cannot claim to regret, I made the most expensive purchase of my clothes-shopping career – a pair of shiny turquoise boots with gold stiletto heels from Gina – I knew there was no chance of pretending they were from Dolcis.

> **'When three tops take a wedge out of the account, our partners may be justified in questioning our logical skills'**

It is not that we genuinely believe our partners have the right to query our purchases but women are seemingly born with a winning combination of guilt and guile which causes us to feel ashamed of being so demonstrably self-indulgent, yet enables us to go ahead anyway, then hide the evidence. ...

adapted from *Daily Express*, 2 January 2002

Before you answer part (a) of the example question, try these activities, which will help you understand the assessment objectives.

Activity 1.15

Focus on *fact* and *opinion*. Remember the definitions on page 10.

Sometimes it's difficult to tell fact from opinion because writers present opinions as if they were facts. Think about these statements:

a) Vegetarians are not supposed to eat meat products.
b) A vegetarian diet is better for children than eating meat.
c) There are fewer vegetarians than there are meat eaters.
d) Meat eating is barbaric and the cause of unnecessary suffering.
e) Eating meat is wrong.
f) My sister is a vegetarian.
g) I think it is better to be vegetarian but I'm not going to do it.

Discuss these with a partner. Try to decide which are facts and which are opinions.

Activity 1.16

Focus on *fact* and *opinion*. Remember the definitions on page 10.

Look at this statement from the article 'Shopping: It's a guy thing': 'The key difference between the sexes is that one "goes shopping" and the other "does the shopping".'

1   Explain how this statement is presented as a fact.
2   Why does the writer want to present it as a fact?
3   Do you think it is a fact? Explain.
4   What is the writer's purpose in making this statement, do you think?

Now answer part (a) of the example question:

a)   What are the main points being made in the article 'Shopping: it's a guy thing'?

Examiners' advice

- In the exam you need to:
    - quickly locate the relevant pieces and re-read them – do not refer to any of the other pieces; just those referred to in the question
    - think carefully about what you learned and discussed about the relevant pieces
    - work through each part of the question in turn
    and most important:
    - answer the question which has been asked, no more and no less.
- Your response should be a combination of your own words, some words paraphrased from the text and some quotation.

PROMPTS

General points to think about and note down

▶ Write down the main topic of the story – the abstract on the top left will give you the answer.

▶ Think about the audience and purpose of the article.

▶ The article is making a number of observations about men's attitude to shopping. Work out how many main points are being made.

▶ Note that some of the writing is clearly observable facts, but some is obviously the writers' opinions.

▶ Write down the topic sentence from each paragraph or section.

▶ Write down some key phrases as quotations as you go through.

Some specific points to consider

▶ Who wrote this article, why and for whom?

▶ What overall and briefly is the article saying?

▶ What was 'odd at the sales last week'?

▶ What may seem unbelievable to most women?

▶ Which points are obviously opinion and which are true facts in the article?

▶ Where have the writers obtained material for their story?

▶ What types of shopping are referred to in the story?

▶ How do the writers use statistics?

Combine these notes and responses as continuous prose.

Approaches to part (b) of the example question

This section will teach you about:

● understanding the content of the articles

● selecting quotations as evidence that you have engaged with and understood the articles

● comparing and contrasting the style of the articles and making cross-references.

Before you answer part (b) of the example question, try these activities, which will help you understand the assessment objectives.

Activity 1.17

Focus on *contrasting style*.

The style of an article or headline really means the manner in which it is written, the tone it creates (see the definition on page 19). The words you would use to describe the style of an article might include:

serious	humorous
flippant	morbid
light-hearted	solemn
thoughtful	frivolous
irreverent	lively

Think of some more words to describe style like those above.

Activity 1.18

Focus on *contrasting style*.

Look at the title and the first two paragraphs from the article in *The Scotsman* and the article by Robert Hardman.

1   Which word or words from the list above would you use to describe each title?
2   Why do you think your word fits?
3   Each article refers to terrorism.

   a)   How does Hardman refer to terrorism in his first paragraph?
   b)   Is it a serious, grave reference or would you describe it another way?

4   Would you say the language used in *The Scotsman* article was flippant or light-hearted? Explain.
5   Which phrases from Hardman's article stand out for you?
6   Which words from the list above best fit this style of writing.

Now answer part (b) of the example question:

b)   Compare the leading article from *The Scotsman* and the article by Robert Hardman in terms of content and style.

Examiners' advice

●   Remember: you are only being asked about the text, not about the pictures, headlines, etc.
●   Remember to compare and make cross-references between the articles.
●   You need to show that you have understood the texts and that you have engaged with them.
●   You need to show some appreciation of the journalistic styles being used.
●   You need to be very obviously comparing the two texts.

PROMPTS

General points to think about and note down

►   Write down what *The Scotsman* story is about in your own words. Include two or three brief quotes to tie your remarks to the text.
►   Write down what the Hardman story is about in your own words. Include some quotations which cover his main points.

►   Note any similarities and differences in content, material, place, time, events reported between the two pieces.
►   Look carefully at the way the stories are written – they are not the same style, each has a different approach. How have the journalists gone about their task differently? Write down your notes.

continued

PROMPTS *continued*

Some specific points to consider

► What is the important word in the title of *The Scotsman* article?

► What is happening to sales in Britain? Against what background?

► What is the leader writer's possible explanation for what is happening?

► How does he develop his explanation in the third paragraph?

► What is 'woefully short' and 'storing up big trouble'?

► What does 'resilient economic performance' mean?

► What 'will be the big issue of 2002'?

► What is implied that we should be doing?

► What is Hardman's point about recession?

► What was happening in Thurrock?

► What, briefly, was the experience of independent jewellers Emson-Haig?

► Who takes a 'stoical view of the economy' and what does he mean?

► How does Hardman use statistics?

► What is his topic conclusion?

Some specific points to consider for comparison and contrast

► What is similar in the writers' descriptions of what people have been doing?

► Are statistics used to make similar points? How?

► Is there anything similar in the conclusions of the articles?

► Is there an implied similarity in the dangers to what we have all been doing?

► Is there a difference in tone between the pieces? Explain.

► Is one piece easier to read, less dense in meaning, more flippant than the other? How?

Some more difficult points to consider

► What is the essential purpose of the leading article?

► Who are the target audience for each piece?

Combine these notes and responses as continuous prose.

Approaches to part (c) of the example question

This section will teach you about:

● how the writers use language for effect
● the need to keep audience in mind.

Before you answer part (c) of the example question, remind yourself of the following definitions and activities:

● language and effect, page 15, Activities 1.9, 1.10, 1.11
● audience, page 17, Activity 1.12.

Now answer part (c) of the example question:

c) Find and comment on interesting or vivid use of language in any of the stories.

Examiners' advice

- You know that there is a further question on headlines and pictures following this, so restrict your response here to the body of the texts.
- Quote examples from the text; one word or short phrase examples are the best.
- Select the best, widest range, most challenging examples and offer a comment or an analysis of them.
- Remember that short phrases and single words get the most marks; large chunks of text are inappropriate here.
- Remind yourself what is required in a question which asks you to comment and analyse – see page 127.

PROMPTS

General points to think about and note down

- Look for the use of cliché, aphorism and other predictable catch phrases; note them down (see Activity 1.10).
- Look for any rhetorical devices; note them down.
- Look for any difficult ideas, concepts, phrases of a technical kind.
- Find and write down interesting or vivid verbs adjectives and adverbs as single words or phrases
- Make reference to the writers' sense of audience and the purpose of his or her writing
- Explain or analyse how and why the writer has chosen the language he has used.

Some specific words and phrases to analyse and comment on

- Make a general comment on the over-use of cliché – what does this tell you about the assumptions being made by writers about their audience?

▶ From 'Darkness at heart of consumer spending spree':

'darkness', 'sombre', 'cruising into 2002', 'spending surge', 'previous assumptions' 'big ticket items', 'personal pension provision', 'resilient', 'darker explanation', 'incentive to save'

▶ From 'In the Retail Temple, worshipping frantically':

'stalking these halls', 'mighty temple to the god of retail', 'two FA Cup final crowds', 'gawping, shuffling peoplescape', 'bedlam', 'sharp-elbowed Essex girls'

▶ From 'Shopping: it's a guy thing':

'dragged along on pain of death', 'Christmas indulgence', 'high street stores, waking up to his spending power', 'hobby shopping'.

Combine these notes and responses as continuous prose.

Approaches to part (d) of the example question

This section will teach you about:

- how the writers use presentational devices
- how pictures, headlines and captions are related and why they are selected
- the intention and effect of presentational devices on the audience of readers.

Before you answer part (d) of the example question, remind yourself of the following definition and activities:

● presentational devices, page 19, Activities 1.13, 1.14.

Now answer part (d) of the example question:

d) Explain the purpose and effect of the headlines, sub-headings, captions and pictures presented in the material.

Examiners' advice

Remember, you are the audience. The writer, photographer and editor have you in mind when the story is put together so refer to this in your comments.

PROMPTS

General points to think about and note down

► Look at all of the headlines first and see which stand out and ask yourself why; it might be size of letters, the words used, the position on the page, or all three.

► Do the same thing with the pictures.

► Remember that the super-headings or abstract (the writing above the headline), the sub-headings (below the main headline or between paragraphs) and the photograph captions are also important.

► Don't be afraid to make some obvious statements, but try to find interesting or subtle meanings or connections between the headlines, stories and pictures.

► Where there are combinations of presentational devices, deal with them altogether so that you can show the links and connections between them.

Some specific points to consider

► From 'Shopping: it's a guy thing':
  – What does the picture show?
  – What is printed on the bags? Comment on this.
  – Comment on the 'guy's' expression.
  – Is there movement (action) in the picture? What is the picture meant to convey to the reader in terms of mood and tone?
  – What does the 'o' in shopping mean? Comment on the relative size of the picture/headline/story.
  – The feature is called 'Focus'. Why?
  – What sort of 'guy' is this? What does that tell you about the editor's view of his audience?
  – From what sub-group of language does the phrase 'it's a guy thing' come? What does this tell you about audience and purpose?
  – Do you think this presentation is successful? Why?

► From 'The first casualty of shopping is the truth':
  – What does the title mean? Of what else is truth the first casualty or victim?

continued on page 34

PROMPTS *continued*

- What does the use of the word 'hubby' tell you about assumptions the writer is making about her audience?
- What does the picture show?
- What is written on the bags? Has this been engineered (done deliberately)? Why?
- What is the function of the quotations on each side of the picture?
- Comment on the suggestion that the woman in the picture does not belong to the rest of the picture.
- Is there any intended humour in the picture?
- Comment on the similarity in composition between this picture and the one from 'Guy thing'.
- How important do you think colour is in the photograph?

Combine your notes and responses as continuous prose.

Check your answer

1 When you have completed your answer to the example question:
   a) check that you have satisfied all the assessment objectives for reading (see page viii)
   b) look at the mark scheme for reading media texts on page ix – which mark band do you think your answer is in? Explain why.
2 If your teacher marks your answer, consider his or her comments and how your mark fits in the mark scheme. Which mark band is your answer in? Can you see why?
3 Consider what you could try to do to move into a higher mark band.

Practice 3

In this section, there are five media items on the topic of winter and an example question, as before. There are fewer prompts to help you than in *Practice 2* but they will help guide your answers. Again, you will have to write the answers yourself.

Example question

Read the five articles on pages 36–40 and study the pictures, headlines and captions:

> *Britain shivers at end of record-breaking warm year*
> *The fun and the fury*
> *Snow and gales cut power and cause chaos*
> *Cold weather kills thousands*
> *Gales sweep in after snowfalls*

and then make a written response to the following questions.

a) What are the main points being made in the article 'Britain shivers at the end of record-breaking warm year'? (Assessment objectives i, ii, iii)

b) Compare the news story, 'Snow and gales cut power and cause chaos' and the article 'Cold weather kills thousands' in terms of content, writing style and purpose. (Assessment objectives i, iv)

c) Find and comment on some interesting or vivid uses of language in any of the stories. (Assessment objective v)

d) Explain the purpose and effect of the pictures, the captions and headlines included in these stories. (Assessment objective v)

Assessment objectives

The assessment objectives are given for each part of the question so you can see:

- why the question has been asked
- what the examiners are looking for in your answer.

Go back to page viii to remind yourself of the assessment objectives.

Approaches to part (a) of the example question

a) What are the main points being made in the article 'Britain shivers at the end of record-breaking warm year'?

Britain shivers at end of record-breaking warm year

TRY to forget the gales and blizzards that are sweeping Britain. End-of-year records show that 2001 was the second-warmest year since records began – and experts predict next year will be even warmer, *writes Tom Robbins.*

The average global temperature in 2001 was 0.42C above the 1961–1991 average. The warmest year since 1860 was 1998, which was 0.57C above the 1961–1990 average.

More significantly, the rise in temperature seems to be a persistent trend. Nine of the 10 warmest years since 1860 came after 1990.

In Britain the high temperatures have led to a delayed autumn, with leaves staying on trees well into December. Last October was the warmest on record, with an average temperature in central England of 13.3C, 2.7C above the 1961–1990 average. There were no hard frosts before mid-December, when temperatures began to fall.

The warm autumn produced other bizarre effects. A cherry tree in west London began to blossom in early December, when a swallow was spotted in Rhyl, north Wales. Swallows normally migrate south in October.

Scientists are wary of saying that current changes in temperature are evidence of global warming, because there have been groups of warm years in the past. This year has actually been colder in Britain than 1949, although the global temperature was higher.

"You cannot infer a trend from one year in isolation, or a short series of years," said a Met Office spokesman. "Drawing too-broad conclusions about climate change is not justified at this stage."

Nevertheless, the weather appears increasingly to be differing from usual patterns. Earlier this month the Met Office reported that the weather in Europe had become "topsy-turvy". In

> ‘A cherry tree flowered in London in December, and a swallow was spotted in Rhyl ’

Thessaloniki in northern Greece, temperatures plunged to below –5C, when the average for this time of year is usually 4C. Iceland recorded 10C when the temperature is normally –5C.

Barcelona and large swathes of southern Europe were hit by severe snow storms, while ski resorts such as Val d'Isère in the French Alps were starved of snow.

Rain patterns in Britain are also inconsistent. For the second year, southeastern regions have received 20% more rain than average, while in northwest England – usually the wettest part of the country – some places received 25% less than average. Armagh and Sutherland had 66% of normal rain, while Cambridgeshire had 132% and Essex 128%.

The Met Office predicts 2002 will be 0.47C above the average temperature, but says it is unlikely to be as hot a year as 1998 was.

This weekend's forecast is less cheering. Snowfalls and freezing temperatures continued in Scotland and parts of northern England last night, with forecasters warning anybody venturing outside to celebrate the new year to dress for sub-zero conditions. In Aberdeen, a rave this weekend that had been expected to attract 7,000 people was cancelled over fears that scantily clad clubbers could become hypothermic.

The Guardian

The fun and the fury

Big freeze sets in for the New Year

WINTRY gales and blizzards will cause disruption across the country, with New Year revellers in the North facing dangerously cold weather, forecasters have warned.

Scotland and Northern Ireland will face the brunt of the weather, although snow is expected as far south as the Midlands and Wales.

Road safety experts are warning the combination of early snow and icy conditions could result in a number of accidents as people begin returning from their Christmas holidays.

Waves crash on to the beach at Seaburn, Sunderland, left, while, above, Cara Faith, 10, and her brother Daniel, two, frolic in the snow at Broughshane, Co. Antrim.

The Guardian, 30 December 2001

Snow and gales cut power and cause chaos

By Gillian Harris and Adam Fresco

Children making the most of the snow in Aberdeen yesterday. Weather forcasters predict that another ten inches will fall over the weekend

THOUSANDS of homes were left without electricity yesterday and roads were closed as gales and blizzards hit many parts of Britain.

The worst affected areas were in Scotland, with forecasters predicting that another ten inches of snow would fall over the weekend.

Motorists were warned to check their routes before travelling today or tomorrow and heavy snow showers were predicted in the north of England across Cumbria to Northum-berland and the eastern coast.

Vera Petrova, from Moscow, wraps up in London

As temperatures fall over the weekend, ice will make untreated roads treacherous. Many minor accidents delayed commuters yesterday as emergency services worked to clear fallen trees from roads in the north of England and north and west Scotland.

In the Cairngorms, deep banks of snow were credited with saving the lives of two climbers who survived a 700ft fall from the summit of a 3,500ft mountain. The two, a man and his wife from Guildford, Surrey, fell down a vertical rock face on Thursday when the snow overhang they were standing on collapsed.

The couple are experienced hillwalkers who were roped together. They landed at the foot of Corrie an Sneachda in fresh snow which cushioned their fall. The woman used her mobile phone to call the Cairngorm mountain rescue team after she discovered that her hus-band had injured his leg. Strong winds made it impossible to use a helicopter, but rescuers carried the man off the mountain on a stretcher.

John Allen, leader of the Cairngorm mountain rescue team, said: 'The first part of the fall was pretty vertical and they would be hitting snow and ice and rocks. Luckily there was a lot of soft new snow at the bottom and this absorbed a lot of the impact. The soft snow also prevented them careering to the bottom, where they might have smashed their heads on ice and rocks."

Temperatures will dip to freezing in most parts of the country over the weekend.

An AA spokesman said: "Motorists need to check the weather for their route before travelling this weekend and give themselves plenty of time to reach their destination. In the areas where there is heavy snow you need to consider whether you have to travel."

He warned motorists travelling through snow to carry warm clothing, spades and chocolate and to ensure that their phones were working. "One of the problems at this time of year is people going away, travelling to areas they are not familiar with," he said.

The Sunday Times, 30 December 2001

Cold weather kills thousands

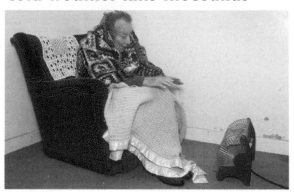

One of thousands of pensioners facing a cold winter

More elderly people die from the cold in London than anywhere else in Europe, according to a study.

Research carried out by London University shows that elderly people living in the British capital are more likely to die from the effects of cold than those living in the coldest parts of Scandinavia.

Their study suggests that 26,596 people die from the effects of cold weather in London every year.

This compares to just over 2,000 people in Finland, where winter temperatures are twice as cold.

The average winter temperature in London is five degrees compared with minus five degrees in Finland.

The researchers suggest that death rates among old people could be reduced if there were improved measures to help old people protect themselves during the winter months.

> " It is a complete scandal and it is the product of years and years of neglect "
>
> Nick Raynsford,
> Minister for London

Poor housing

Paula Jones from Age Concern, said the problem was caused by poor housing.

"The main reason is that we have not invested over the years in good, well-insulated housing and now the poorest older people are living in the poorest housing which is badly insulated, hard and expensive to heat."

Nick Raynsford, Minister for London, told the BBC that the death rates were scandalous.

"Yes, it is a complete scandal and it is the product of years and years of neglect.

"That is exactly why the government is acting to tackle these problems.

"We accept entirely there is an acute problem and we want to sort it out."

He said the government was giving extra money to poorer pensioners to help them to heat their homes over winter and was also carrying out a modernisation programme to improve existing homes.

He added that changes to building regulations would ensure future homes were more energy efficient and were easier to heat.

Nevertheless, thousands of elderly people will spend the winter at home without heating. Many will die.

adapted from BBC News website:
ttp://news.bbc.co.uk/hi/english/health

Taking cover: a woman and child walk through Kelvingrove Park, Glasgow, yesterday as up to 4in of snow fell on Scotland

Gales sweep in after snowfalls

By Russell Jenkins and Linus Gregoriadis

SEVERE gales reaching 70mph were forecast to hit southern and north-west England early today.

Peter Stewart, for the Meteorological Office, said: "It will be very windy across the Irish Sea, the Bristol Channel and the English Channel. The gales will be strongest near coasts and in hilly areas." The storms are expected to die down by tomorrow.

The gales follow snowfalls over parts of northern England and Scotland yesterday. More than 20 schools in Fife closed early because of the weather. Up to 4in of snow fell on high ground in north-east Scotland. It proved to be a bad day for the opening of a £1.4 million work of art in Newcastle upon Tyne – the "blue carpet" of 22,500 crystal tiles outside the Laing Art Gallery was hidden by snow.

In Cornwall, a body was recovered from the entrance to Porthleven harbour. The unnamed man was the third person to die in storms around the Cornish coast this week.

In South Devon, 15 dead dolphins and two porpoises have been washed ashore in a week, bringing the total found in Britain to 47 so far this year. Wildlife campaigners believe many died after being caught in fishing nets.

The Times, 26 January 2002

SPECIFIC PROMPTS TO ANSWER ON YOUR OWN

▶ What does the writer say, generally, about the trend of average global temperatures?

▶ How is this reflected in Britain? Refer to statistics and examples.

▶ What should not be inferred from these facts and what, nevertheless, is interesting about weather trends?

▶ What, briefly, does the writer say about rainfall and the weather forecast?

▶ What light-hearted point does he make at the end of his article?

▶ How does the writer mix fact and opinion in the article? Give brief examples.

Write your responses as continuous prose.

Approaches to part (b) of the example question

b) Compare the story 'Snow and gales cut power and cause chaos' and the article 'Cold weather kills thousands' in terms of content, writing style and purpose.

SPECIFIC PROMPTS TO ANSWER ON YOUR OWN

▶ What sort of story is 'Snow and gales ...'? What information does it give you?

   – How many 'sections' could you say the story has?

   – For what purpose is the Cairngorms incident related?

   – Does the piece give advice in any way? How?

   – Do the writers involve (draw in) their readers? How?

▶ What is the main point of the 'Cold weather kills ...' story?

   – Is there a moral point being made? What is it?

   – Does the writer involve or draw in his readers more than the Cairngorms story? How? Why?

   – What is the purpose of the story and who is it aimed at?

   – Comment in any way on the views expressed by the government minister

▶ What differences in tone, purpose, reporting style, layout and effect are there between the two articles?

▶ Are there any differences in the use of words between the two articles?

▶ Which story are you likely to remember longest? Why?

Write your responses as continuous prose.

Approaches to part (c) of the example question

c) Find and comment on some interesting or vivid uses of language in any of the stories.

SPECIFIC PROMPTS TO ANSWER ON YOUR OWN

► In 'Britain shivers at end of record-breaking warm year' there are some uses of metaphor and vivid expressions.

► How would you describe and explain the level of language used by Harris and Fresco in their story?

► For what purpose has the minister chosen his words in 'Cold weather kills …'?

► Comment on some of the words used in the headlines and picture captions.

Write your responses as continuous prose.

Approaches to part (d) of the example question

d) Explain the purpose and effect of the six pictures included in these stories.

SPECIFIC PROMPTS TO ANSWER ON YOUR OWN

► What is the relationship between the title 'The fun and the fury' and the pictures?

► What is the purpose and effect of the pictures with 'Snow and gales cut power and cause chaos'? How do the pictures relate to the story?

► What is the relevance of the picture of Vera Petrova?

► What do you think the thinking was behind the picture editor's decision to use the picture he chose for 'Cold weather kills …'?

► What has the editor used instead of a picture in the story 'Britain shivers at end of record-breaking warm year'?

► Comment on the 'umbrellas' picture.

Write your responses as continuous prose

Check your answer

1 When you have completed your answer to the example question:
   a) check that you have satisfied all the assessment objectives for reading (see page viii)
   b) look at the mark scheme for reading media texts on page ix – which mark band do you think your answer is in? Explain why.
2 If your teacher marks your answer, consider his or her comments and how your mark fits in the mark scheme. Which mark band is your answer in? Can you see why?
3 Consider what you could try to do to move into a higher mark band.

Practice 4

In this final *Practice* section, you are given the instruction and question just as you would be in an examination … and you are on your own.

Specimen examination question

Paper 1, Section A: Media

Question 1

Read the four articles on pages 45–8 and study the pictures, headlines and captions:

> *Gales bring flooding and power cuts* by Hamida Ghafour
> *When the weather goes like a bomb* by Paul Simons
> *Flooding alerts rise as storms sweep in* by Tim Teeman
> *Boy, 14, saves woman as car is swept away* by Kirsty Turner

and then make a written response to the following questions.

a) What are the main points being made in the article 'Gales bring flooding and power cuts'?

b) Compare the article 'When the weather goes like a bomb' by Paul Simons with the news story 'Flooding alerts rise as storms sweep in' by Tim Teeman

c) Comment on how the language in 'Boy, 14, saves woman as car is swept away' by Kirsty Turner makes the report dramatic.

d) Explain the purpose and effect of the headlines, sub-headings, captions and pictures presented in the material.

Write a full answer in continuous prose.

Check your answer

1   When you have completed your answer to the specimen examination question:
   a) check that you have satisfied all the assessment objectives for reading (see page viii)
   b) look at the mark scheme for reading media texts on page ix – which mark band do you think your answer is in? Explain why.
2   If your teacher marks your answer, consider his or her comments and how your mark fits in the mark scheme. Which mark band is your answer in? Can you see why?
3   Consider what you could try to do to move into a higher mark band.

Gales bring flooding and power cuts

Surf's up: waves hit Selsey, West Sussex. Nearby, a cross-Channel ferry ran aground on a sandbank

On your marks: a woman makes a run for it in the wind in Brighton

BY HAMIDA GHAFOUR

Transport and power services were disrupted and homes flooded as winds of up to 90mph and rain lashed Britain yesterday.

The Environmental Protection Agency put the whole of the west coast on flood watch and storms knocked out power lines, halted rail services and caused a ferry to run aground.

The strongest winds were recorded in Dartmoor and in Stornoway in the Outer Hebrides. At least 66 flood warnings were issued throughout Britain, with Wales suffering the most. Six homes at Carmarthen Quay were flooded by tidal surges washing over the sea wall.

Tidal surges along the western coastline were as high as 30ft, in some places the highest for four years.

Police closed the promenade in Blackpool as huge waves pounded the sea wall. Several cars were stranded after motorists ignored police warnings and tried to drive through water several feet deep.

DAMAGE

Three people were caught off guard by the flooded River Severn near Gloucester. They ended up stranded in their vehicles, including one man who scrambled on to the roof of his van to await rescue.

The bad weather meant more misery for people in areas affected by storms at the beginning of the week when millions of pounds' worth of damage was caused.

DAY OFF

Hundreds of homes in Scotland were without power for most of the day. Children in the Western Isles were given the day off school because the winds were so bad.

The main West Coast railway line from Scotland to England was shut after power lines were damaged. Many ferry services were affected. Sailings from Stranraer to Belfast were cancelled.

A cross-Channel ferry from Dieppe to Newhaven with 72 passengers on board ran aground on a sandbank off East Sussex after winds blew the vessel off course. A tug tried to pull it free but the captain managed to swing the ferry around and headed back to sea when the tide rose. No one was hurt.

UNSCATHED

A westerly wind battered the coast from Merseyside to Cumbria but the eastern side of Britain was relatively unscathed. A spokesman for the EPA said: "The high tides, combined with the strong winds are pushing water against the barriers. But in East Anglia, the wind is actually blowing the tide off the coast."

Ten pieces of metal, each 15ft by 4ft, were torn away. Police cordoned off a large area of the shopping centre. Sancha Tetlow, a forecaster at the Met Office, said: "This wasn't as bad as the storms we saw on Monday but this was still a bad winter storm. There has been a lot of cars blown over by winds, trees overturned.

"It's a low, deep pressure system in the Atlantic that's causing these winds. It's moving through the North-West to Scotland."

The winds are expected to die down over the weekend although there will be some rain. Temperatures will be around 10C to 12C.

"Winds will abate by Sunday but rain will be the main issue," said the Met Office.

adapted from *The Daily Telegraph*, 2 February 2002

Seaside break: trams on Blackpool seafront had to be towed to safety as gales and high tides swept along the northwest coast yesterday

When the weather goes like a bomb

Paul Simons

Weather Correspondent

THE storms battering Britain have been the most violent for several years.

A weather 'bomb' – a monster that can grow from an ordinary depression to hurricane strength in 12 to 24 hours – has been sweeping in from the Atlantic.

Such storms intensify faster than 24 millibars in a day. The storms we are experiencing are deepening to about 50 millibars in the same time.

This explosion of power makes them especially dangerous to shipping, which is why crossing the Irish Sea this weekend will be nerve-wracking. Wales, southwest and southeast of England and northwest Scotland are also on alert for winds gusting to 70mph, heavy rain and localised flooding.

The devastating storms of January 1953, October 1987 and Burns Night 1990 were all "bombs", but not all their damage was caused by winds. In the storm of 1953, the intense low pressure sucked up a huge bulge of water in the North Sea which was funnelled down into the English Channel in a storm surge. On top of a high tide, sea rose 20ft to 30ft and broke the sea defences along the coast of East Anglia and the Thames Estuary, killing more than 300 people. In the Netherlands, about 2,000 drowned.

This weekend, coastal defences will again be tested, and flood warnings have been issued for the coastlines of Ireland, southwest England and southwest Scotland.

The storms of the past week have been typical North Atlantic winter depressions. They are born from a titanic clash between warm tropical air swept up along the Gulf Stream and cold air pouring from Canada and Greenland. Warm and cold air do not mix, and the bigger temperature difference, the more violent the struggle between them.

They spin round in a depression and the warm air rises up rapidly through the middle of the storm, driving the winds faster. The warm tropical air trapped inside the depression explains the incredibly mild temperatures during our present storms – today's temperatures will reach 54F (12C).

The battle between warm and cold air masses also creates a strong jet stream several miles above the ground.

This ribbon of wind is now roaring at full speed, and like an overhead railway is dragging the storms northwest across the Atlantic, which is why northwest Scotland is bearing the brunt.

The worst of the present weather may not be over yet. Each storm sets off a daughter storm in its wake, rather like the way whirlpools spin off a stick dragged through the surface on a pond.

So for the next few days at least, we can expect more rain, wind and flooding.

The Times, 2 February 2002

Flooding alerts rise as storms sweep in

By Tim Teeman

A SHIP ran aground, ferries were cancelled and motorists were forced to abandon their cars as extreme weather continued yesterday.

Up to 25,000 people across Britain and Ireland were left without electricity and the stormy conditions caused a catalogue of accidents, with southern and western areas hardest hit. Gusts of 82mph were recorded on the Hebridean island of South Uist, and 72mph in Mumbles, South Wales.

Storms, strong winds and severe floods will continue to wreak havoc this weekend, although the storms are expected to be less severe than Monday's, which caused eight deaths and millions of pounds in damage. Drivers are advised only to make journeys when absolutely necessary.

FLOODING

A Met Office spokesman said: "Some areas in the West have seen the worst of this latest spell, but looking east we are giving warnings of severe gales and heavy rain in Greater London, Surrey and Hertfordshire." Last night the Environment Agency issued 28 "flood watches" – areas where flooding was "possible" – in England and 40 in Wales. There were 69 "flood warnings" – areas where flooding was "expected, affecting businesses and homes" – in England and Wales.

In Newhaven, East Sussex, 17 passengers and 52 crew were stranded for three hours when the passenger ship *Sardinia Vira* ran aground outside the port because of high winds. The ship eventually made it safely into port. In Wales, rugby fans on their way to the international against Ireland in Dublin were stranded at ports in South Wales because of strong winds.

Coastguards warned farmers to move livestock in low-lying coastal regions to higher ground after a woman farmer was almost drowned trying to stop her sheep being swept out to sea near Kirby-in-Furness, Cumbria. She clung to a hedge and was rescued by coastguards and taken to hospital suffering from hypothermia. The flock drowned.

RESCUE

A man was rescued from a crumbling sea wall in Greenodd, Cumbria. Coastguards saved two people from a car that had become flooded at Glen Capel on the River Nith near Dumfries. Near Gloucester three drivers were rescued from vehicles after a lane was flooded by the River Severn.

Police closed Blackpool seafront amid 20ft waves and 30 people were escorted from the South Pier. A man was rescued from a Blackpool pumping station as water levels rose. Peter Croft, engineering services manager for Blackpool Council, said: "There is a big-clean up operation here. There is a lot of debris now all over the seafront, tram tracks and promenade."

Waves broke sea defences in Bideford, Devon, flooding the main streets. Annie Brenton, the mayor, said: "we're in the process of building our flood defences. I look forward to the day they're in place".

In Scotland severe flood warnings were issued for the Teviot in the Borders and the Earn, Perth and Kinross.

The Times, 2 February 2002

BOY, 14, SAVES WOMAN AS CAR IS SWEPT AWAY

A 14-YEAR-OLD BOY has been hailed a hero after rescuing an hysterical woman from her car just minutes before it was swept into the sea.

Daniel ... shouted at the screaming woman to force her out of the Morris Minor, which had broken down after being swamped by a wave ... near Penzance, on Friday evening.

'I'm just glad that the woman got out,' said the school pupil from Penzance. 'If she hadn't I don't think she'd be here today.'

Daniel was with a group of about six friends on the way to a birthday party when they heard shouting from the stricken vehicle.

A male passenger was already out of the car and standing in waist-high water.

Daniel's friends, both 14, stayed on dry land and held onto the car to prevent it being swept into the sea by huge waves and high winds, while Daniel jumped into the sea.

'I tried to help the man push the car onto dry land, but it was very difficult because waves were hitting against it,' he said.

'I shouted to the man to get his wife out of the car because she was still sitting in the driving seat. He

By KIRSTY TURNER

shouted at her but she was in a state of shock, so I went around to the side of the car and shouted at her to get out for goodness sake. Eventually she did and made it out of the water.

'I got out then and shouted to the man to get out and save his life and leave the car. I think they'd only bought it two days before, but eventually he did.'

The vehicle was then hit by another wave and swept into the sea where it sank just after police and coastguards arrived.

Alarm

They had been alerted by a female friend of Daniel's who had raised the alarm on her mobile phone.

'I didn't really think what I was doing at the time, I just wanted to help the woman,' said Daniel. 'She was very shocked and upset and the man was very frustrated at not being able to get the car out. I did hold onto the car so that if anything had happened I could have hauled myself onto the sidewalk.

'I don't really think of myself as a

hero. My friends played a part in it as well.'

A male passer-by also helped in the rescue and everyone escaped unhurt.

'I thought they were all marvellous,' said Daniel's mum. 'Considering their ages they all showed an incredible presence of mind and were absolutely brilliant.'

The youngsters even managed to make it to their party.

She laughed: 'Daniel rushed in, gave me this garbled story, got changed out of his wet clothes and went out again.'

Penzance seafront was devastated by the stormy weather, with roads closed due to large waves, rocks and debris washed up and manhole covers lifted by the sea.

A major search was launched to find a man seen larking about on the railings of the promenade as high seas pounded the area and two people had to be pulled out of the sea by coastguards after being washed into the water.

A spokesperson from Devon and Cornwall police, said: 'We are pleading that people should not go to such areas and not put themselves in such danger.'

adapted from *Sunday Independent*, 3 February 2002

2 Reading non-fiction texts

As with the media question, the non-fiction question will be testing some or all of the assessment objectives for reading set out on page viii.

Extracts from a mark scheme for non-fiction texts are set out on pages x–xi.

The *Practice* sections in this chapter use non-fiction texts in exactly the same way as in the examination. You are given help as follows:

- Practice 1, page 50 – the example question is based on an extract from *Neither Here Nor There* by Bill Bryson; prompts and sample responses are provided
- Practice 2, page 58 – the example question is based on an extract from *Grace and Favour* by Jane Lapotaire; prompts are provided
- Practice 3, page 62 – the example question is based on an extract from *Something to Declare* by Julian Barnes; prompts and sample responses are provided
- Practice 4, page 69 – the example question is based on an extract from *Writing Home* by Alan Bennett; prompts are provided
- Practice 5, page 73 – the specimen examination question is based on an extract from *A Mad World My Masters* by John Simpson; this is exactly like the examination – you are given no help at all.

Examiners' advice
- Remember that this part of the exam is 'unseen', which means that you will not see the non-fiction extract on which the question is based until you open the exam paper.
- The extract may be linked to the topic used for media, or it may not.
- The two questions in Section A are separate – **you only refer to the non-fiction piece when answering the non-fiction question.**

Practice 1

In this section you are given lots of help to answer the example question, with prompts and sample responses.

Example question

Read the extract below. It comes from Bill Bryson's travel book *Neither Here Nor There*. In this extract he has travelled to the Arctic Circle in Norway.

• Explain where Bill Bryson is and what he is doing. (Assessment objectives i, iv)

• How does Bryson use language to communicate his experiences in an engaging and vivid way? (Assessment objectives i, ii, iv, v)

Hammerfest

On my sixteenth day in Hammerfest, it happened. I was returning from the headland after my morning walk and in an empty piece of sky above the town there appeared a translucent cloud of many colours – pinks and greens and blues and pale purples. It glimmered and seemed to swirl. Slowly it stretched across the sky. It had an oddly oily quality about it, like the rainbows you sometimes see in pool of petrol. I stood transfixed.

I knew from my reading that the Northern Lights are immensely high up in the atmosphere, something like 200 miles up, but this show seemed to be suspended just above the town. There are two kinds of Northern Light – the curtains of shimmering gossamer that everyone has seen in pictures, and the rather rarer gas clouds that I was gazing at now. They are never the same twice. Sometimes they shoot wraith-like across the sky, like smoke in a wind tunnel, moving at enormous speed and sometimes they hang like luminous drapes or glittering spears of light, and very occasionally – perhaps once or twice in a lifetime, they creep out from every point on the horizon and flow together overhead in a spectacular, silent explosion of light and colour.

In the depthless blackness of the countryside, where you may be a hundred miles from the nearest artificial light, they are capable of the most weird and unsettling optical illusions. They can seem to come out of the sky and fly at you at enormous speeds, as if trying to kill you. Apparently it's terrifying. To this day, many Lapps earnestly believe that if you show the Lights a white handkerchief or a sheet of white paper they will come and take you away.

This display was relatively small stuff, and it lasted for only a few minutes, but it was the most beautiful thing I had ever seen and it would do me until something better came along.

In the evening, something did – a display of Lights that went on for hours. They were of only one colour, that eerie luminous green you see on radar screens, but the activity was frantic. Narrow swirls of light would sweep across the great dome of sky, then hang there like vapour trails. Sometimes they flashed across the sky like falling stars and sometimes they spun languorously, reminding me of the lazy way smoke used to rise from my father's pipe when he was reading. Sometimes the Lights would flicker brightly in the west, then vanish in an instant and reappear a moment later behind me, as if teasing me. I was constantly turning and twisting to see it. You have no idea how immense the sky is until you try to monitor it all. The eerie thing was how silent it was. Such activity seemed to demand at the very least an occasional low boom or a series of static-like crackles, but there was none. All this immense energy was spent without a sound.

I was very cold – inside my boots I wore three pairs of socks but still my toes were numb and I began to worry about frostbite – but I stayed and watched for perhaps two hours, unable to pull myself away.

There are two parts to the question:

● the first part asks for basic *understanding* of the text
● the second is about the *language* used. The second part of the question requires detailed, close reading and appreciation of the text; this is where the highest marks are.

Assessment objectives

The assessment objectives are given for each part of the question so you can see:

● why the question has been asked
● what the examiners are looking for in your answer.

Go back to page viii to remind yourself of the assessment objectives.

Examiners' advice

● You will certainly have to read the passage at least twice before you attempt to write your answer to the question. Your first reading should be at your normal reading speed, without stopping to consider each point closely, picking up the general idea. Closer reading – looking for specific ways of answering the question – comes later. As you read the piece for the first time, consider the tone (see the definition on page 19).

- When you come to write your answer to the question there is, of course, no need to deal with each part of the question separately. You may do so if you wish, but it is actually often easier to deal with them both at the same time. When you write about the content (first bullet point), it is very difficult to do so without referring to the language (second bullet point), and vice versa.

Approaches to the first part of the example question

Before you answer the first part of the example question, remind yourself of the following definitions and activities:

- engaging with and interpreting text, page 9, Activities 1.1, 1.2
- fact and opinion, page 10, Activities 1.4, 1.5.

Now answer the first part of the example question:

- Explain where Bill Bryson is and what he is doing.

PROMPTS

- ▶ Go through the article noting references to where Bryson is, what time of day it is, references to places.
- ▶ Write down, and quote, anything written about the surroundings referred to in the passage.
- ▶ What are the Northern Lights?
- ▶ What was the weather like? What other general conditions are referred to?

- ▶ Explain, generally, what Bryson is doing – what is his job?
- ▶ Make some comments about the **genre** of travel writing.
- ▶ Comment on Bryson's feelings, reactions and attitude to what he is doing and where he is
- ▶ Remember to use brief, appropriate quotations.

Definition

Genre describes the different types of writing which have their own features, for example travel writing, crime writing, historical writing, newspaper reports, biography.

Possible responses

Here are some responses to the prompts above. Check them against what you found

- We know from the example question that Bryson is in Norway, within the Arctic Circle; he is at a place called Hammerfest. He tells us that he was 'returning from the headland' at the end of his morning walk. He tells us he had been in Hammerfest for 16 days. He has his first Northern Lights experience outside the town, he sees the Lights 'in an empty piece of sky above the town'. Later Bryson had a second experience, this time in the evening.

- An interpretative or insightful comment might be that during Bryson's experiences it was dark all of the time, because of how the seasons are in the Arctic Circle. We also notice his reference to 'Lapps', the people who live in this arctic land.

- Notice that the quotations used here are woven into the writing. This is an effective way of quoting briefly. Longer quotes would be separated and centred.

- You need to explain briefly what the Northern Lights are. You could just say that they are a famous natural phenomenon of coloured light which appear either as swirling clouds or as hanging curtains. Choose two or three phrases from the text which captures the colour or activity of the Lights.

- Mention of the headland allows us to interpret that Hammerfest is probably on the coast, there is a sense of openness and vastness in 'the great dome of sky' and referring to the sky as 'immense'. It is very cold and it is silent, a silence described as 'eerie'.

- Bryson has travelled to Hammerfest because he is a professional travel writer. We may conclude that he has travelled to northern Norway specifically to see the Lights because he seems to have been waiting 16 days for something to happen.

- Travel writing is a genre in its own right. The extract is not telling a story, it is an account of an actual experience and therefore fact not fiction. But you could also mention that it is personal writing and descriptive writing. Bryson writes in the first person, but also uses the second person, 'where you may be a hundred miles'. He is aware of the audience and wants to involve and include his reader in his experience.

- Apart from doing all the things referred to above, Bryson also has feelings, reactions, attitudes about his experiences. There are lots of opinions here, in the form of feelings expressed. This is also what he is doing.

- It may be that after 16 days his enthusiasm is waning, but then 'it happened'. Bryson said that he 'stood transfixed' at the sight of the 'translucent clouds of many colours'. Later he was 'unable to pull himself away' despite oncoming frostbite. The colours, shapes, energy, speed, 'optical illusions' and the 'eerie silence' all suggest that he was overawed, excited, gripped, entertained, astounded and engrossed by the experience. Yet he keeps a professional writer's distance from the event; he is able to include information, **analogy** and controlled descriptive writing in the account of his experience. We get the feeling that it was worth the journey and the wait. You could suggest that, between the lines, Bryson is saying that the experience of this natural and unique phenomenon is an experience everyone should have. Since we can't all go there, the travel writer's job is to provide us with the experience. That is what he is doing.

If you check back you will be able to see that the responses satisfy the assessment objectives.

> **Definition**
>
> An **analogy** is a comparison with something similar which is used to give the reader a clear idea of what the writer is saying. For example, 'sometimes they *spun languorously*, reminding me of the *lazy way smoke used to rise* from my father's pipe when he was reading'.

Approaches to the second part of the question

This section will teach you about:

- how writers use linguistic devices to achieve their effects, and comment on ways language varies and changes
- how to select examples which are appropriate
- how to use some technical terms.

Before you answer the second part of the example question, check that you understand the following definitions and try the activities. They will help you to understand the assessment objectives.

> **Definitions**
>
> - To **analyse** means to examine in detail, to take a close look at, to see which words were chosen and why.
> - To **evaluate** means to make a judgement about, to assess, to appraise whether or not the use of words is successful, effective, helpful, generally good — and why.

Activity 2.1

Focus on *analysing* and *evaluating* the writer's use of language.

1   Read the extract below from the Bill Bryson piece.
2   Write down why you think it is a good piece of writing. Write two or three sentences.

'Sometimes they shoot wraith-like across the sky, like smoke in a wind tunnel, moving at enormous speed and sometimes they hang like luminous drapes or glittering spears of light, and very occasionally – perhaps once or twice in a lifetime, they creep out from every point on the horizon and flow together overhead in a spectacular, silent explosion of light.'

Activity 2.2

Focus on some technical terms.

Remind yourself of the parts of speech:

1   Write a sentence in your own words to define:

   a) a noun
   b) a verb
   c) an adjective
   d) adverb.

2 What is the everyday meaning of the word 'image'?
3 What do writers mean when they write an 'image'?
4 What is the difference between a **simile** and a metaphor?
5 Close your eyes and think of the sky. Try to create some different images of the sky, for example:
   * on a beautiful summer's day
   * on a rainy, windy day
   * during thunder and lightning
   * at sunset ('red sky at night').
   a) List nouns, verbs, adjectives and adverbs to describe your images.
   b) Now write some similes and metaphors to describe those states of the sky.

Definitions

* A **simile** is when a writer compares one thing with another using the words 'as' or 'like' to link them.
* **Assonance** is the deliberate repetition of a vowel sound for effect, usually but not necessarily the first letter, for example, *amber apples hung above the arches*.

Activity 2.3

Focus on *assonance* and *alliteration*. Remember the definition of alliteration on page 22.

Make up some examples of assonance and alliteration of your own.

Activity 2.4

Look again at the extract in Activity 2.1. Using what you have learned in Activities 2.2 and 2.3, comment on the use of language. Use the technical terms you have learned.

Now answer the second part of the question:

* How does Bryson use language to communicate his experiences in an engaging and vivid way?

Examiners' advice

* When you are reading the passage for the third time, you need to do so more slowly, noting specific examples of the way in which the writer has used language for different purposes and effects. You will not be able to write about all of these in the examination, because there simply isn't enough time, so you have to be selective, picking out the most striking examples. Demonstrating a knowledge of some technical terms will also impress the examiner.

- You could answer the second part of the question on language by focusing on one section, say two paragraphs, of the extract.

PROMPTS

Read the first paragraph focusing on the words and their effect.

▶ How does Bryson introduce a sense of expectation into the passage?

▶ How does he describe the 'translucent cloud'?
▶ What specific image does he use?
▶ Explain how Bryson involves the reader in the experiences he is having.

Possible responses

Here are some possible responses to the prompts above. Check them against what you found.

- He uses the phrase 'it happened' as if it was a single, dramatic event, long awaited. The piece of sky is 'empty' as if waiting to be filled with the beauty of the Northern Lights.
- He uses vivid words 'pinks and greens and blues and pale purples'. Notice that these are nouns. He also uses verbs, 'glimmered' and 'seemed to swirl'. So the writer uses colour and movement words.
- Colours are easy to share with readers. The picture he saw in the sky can be created in the reader's mind.

- The phrase 'oddly oily' stands out because of its assonance. The everyday image of the colours in a pool of spilt petrol connects the unique phenomenon of the Northern Lights with something ordinary which we can see almost every day.
- In writing 'like the rainbows you sometimes see', Bryson uses 'you' to directly involve the reader and uses 'rainbow', which is another natural phenomenon but one which most people have experienced. The reader cannot think of a rainbow without thinking of colours. So again, again, colour words are seen to be important.

PROMPTS

Read the second, third and fourth paragraphs carefully.

▶ The language and purpose changes in the second paragraph. Explain how.
▶ Find and explain examples of simile and metaphor used effectively in the second and third paragraphs.

▶ How is the experience of the Lights developed and extended in the third paragraph? Show how the use of language helps this.
▶ Find examples of fact and other examples of opinion in paragraphs two and three.
▶ What are the important phrases in the short fourth paragraph? What is this paragraph doing?

Possible responses

Here are some responses to the prompts above. Check them against what you found.

- The writer connects his experience with what he has read about the Northern Lights. There is information given to the reader; the style is more detached here. He is not trying to enthuse and excite the reader but inform him, give him a knowledge context for the experience of the Lights.

- However there are also vivid, descriptive phrases: 'shimmering gossamer', 'shoot wraith-like', 'luminous drapes or glittering spears' and 'depthless blackness'.

    It would be appropriate to try to explain one or two of these more extended ideas. For example, 'luminous drapes' brings to mind a curtain of cloth hanging down, brightly coloured as if it were transparent with a coloured light shining fiercely through it.

- Choose two or three more descriptive phrases and explain them in your own words to get across the effect of Bryson's language.

- 'they creep out' is a metaphor; 'like smoke in a wind tunnel' is a simile. Find some more. Explain how they work.

- The 'weird and unsettling optical illusions' develop and extend the experience from vivid description to the idea of the Lights 'trying to kill you' or the idea that 'they will come and take you away'. The word 'terrifying' is used. The Lights are no longer an exciting and enjoyable phenomena in this paragraph. They have become a threat, something sinister, especially if you are in the middle of the countryside alone.

- The culture and beliefs of the Lapps is included here with the image of the white handkerchief and the emphasis words, 'earnestly believe'.

- The apparent beliefs of the Lapps is a fact; the height of the Lights at 200 feet is a fact: what the Lights 'seem' to do and how they look to Bryson is opinion.

- Bryson juxtaposes 'small stuff' with 'most beautiful' in this cleverly balanced sentence which also balances the extract. Something even more spectacular is to come.

More things to think about

- Describe what happened in the evening.
- Select words and phrases which vividly and successfully describe the phenomenon.
- Explain some of the descriptive phrases, for example 'swirls of light', 'dome of sky'.
- Name some of the parts of speech and types of imagery used in this part of the extract.
- Explain some of the images in your own words.
- Bryson uses another everyday example to compare with what he is seeing. What is it? How does it work?
- How does Bryson use words and phrases to make his important points about 'silence'?
- Explain the reason for and effect of the last short paragraph.

Select material from your work above and write your answer in continuous prose.

Check your answer

1   When you have completed your answer to the example question:
    a) check that you have satisfied all the assessment objectives for reading (see page viii)
    b) look at the mark scheme for reading non-fiction texts on page x – which mark band do you think your answer is in? Explain why.

2   If your teacher marks your answer, consider his or her comments and how your mark fits in the mark scheme. Which mark band is your answer in? Can you see why?

3   Consider what you could try to do to move into a higher mark band.

Practice 2

In this section you are given prompts to guide you, but you will have to find the answers for yourself.

Example question

Read the extract below. It comes from Jane Lapotaire's autobiography *Grace and Favour*. As a young girl used to living in Ipswich, Jane finds herself visiting some of her family in Libya.

Write about:

- where Jane is and what she is doing   (Assessment objectives i, iv)

- how the writer has used language to create atmosphere for the reader.

                                                         (Assessment objectives i, ii, iv, v)

Hot Night

I coughed. My throat was parched, my body damp with sweat. The sheet stuck to me. I threw it off. It stuck to the sheet under my back. I turned on my side. Then my face sank deep into the pillow. I turned quickly on to my back again splaying my arms and legs so that no part of my body was in contact with my burning flesh. I breathed in for seven and out for seven. Lucky number. That would bring sleep. How could anyone sleep in this heat? The chirping outside the window seemed louder than ever in the darkness.

Irritably, I got out of bed and went to stand by the shuttered windows, almost tripping up on the nightdress that I'd discarded earlier. A dark shape stirred on the floor and sighed. Bebop. I put my thumb in my mouth and wondered if he'd let me play with his ear and snuggle up to him. Better not. He didn't know me. I'm a stranger, I thought.

I stood with my nose up against the gaps in the slats of wood like a dog breathing in the draught under a door.

The breeze was stirring the trees outside, more than it had done earlier. More air inside the room with the shutters open! Brainwave. I switched the bedside light on and went back to inspect the strange-looking catch that held the windows together. Everything was different here. Even catches on windows. No, it wasn't a window. It was a shutter.

I pushed it sideways hard, hoping it wouldn't make a noise. It hardly moved and I barked my knuckles on the wood. I couldn't pull it down any further. It simply wouldn't go. Trickles of sweat made their way down my neck. In growing impatience I pushed it up. It sprang out of my sticky hand with a jerk and then I saw that it had to be pushed sideways to be released from the metal bar in which it was lodged. The shutters folded back like the pleats of a concertina, revealing the inkiness of the night. An arm's length away from the window, two small trees waved their branches slowly, leaves rustling. Tall bushes near them moved in the opposite direction, like a silent ballet. The air felt so good on my face. It wasn't much cooler, but at least it was moving. I felt the sweat on my neck begin to dry. I switched the light off so that I could enjoy the picture-like quality of the night framed by the rim of the window.

I don't know how long I stood there but I was suddenly aware of a cramp-like ache in my knees – my legs were stiff and aching from being in the same position.

I clicked the light back on and got back on to the bed. The sheets, thicker than any I'd seen before, were unbelievably crumpled. There was a damp patch on the bed beside the pillow where I must have sucked my thumb and dribbled.

There are two parts to the question:

- the first part asks for basic *understanding* of the text
- the second is about the *language* used. The second part of the question requires detailed, close reading and appreciation of the text; this is where the highest marks are.

Assessment objectives

The assessment objectives are given for each part of the question so you can see:

- why the question has been asked
- what the examiners are looking for in your answer.

Go back to page viii to remind yourself of the assessment objectives.

Approaches to the first part of the question

Write about:

- where Jane is and what she is doing

Examiners' advice

- Begin, as always, by reading the passage at your normal reading speed
  - to gain a general idea of the content and the tone the writer is using
  - without pausing to consider any point in detail.
- When you have worked through the prompts, go through your notes and add appropriate, short quotations from the text.

PROMPTS

- ▶ What does the question tell you about where Jane is?
- ▶ Inside what sort of room is she? Describe what you can of it.
- ▶ What does the *passage* tell you of her immediate surroundings outside the room?
- ▶ What is the air like, and the atmosphere?

- ▶ What is Jane trying to do? Explain her problem.
- ▶ What actions does Jane take? Why?
- ▶ What does Jane do at the end of the passage?
- ▶ Why do you think Jane does not want to make a noise?

Approaches to the second part of the question

Write about:

- how the writer has used language to create atmosphere for the reader.

PROMPTS

- ▶ Which words and phrases does the writer use to describe the atmosphere in the room and what Jane is feeling? Comment on the words you have chosen.
- ▶ Comment on the length of the sentences. Why are they like this? How does the length if sentences reflect Jane's problem?
- ▶ Which words in the second paragraph show you what mood Jane is in?
- ▶ In the fourth paragraph there are lots of images. Explain, 'I barked my knuckles on the wood'. There are two similes and two metaphors later in this

paragraph. Find them; explain how they work.
- ▶ Which words and phrases does the writer use to describe Jane feeling better, relieved at the end of this paragraph? Quote some and explain.
- ▶ What does the last paragraph tell you about Jane's situation and her age?

More things to think about

- ▶ How has the writer involved you in her experience?
- ▶ Did you feel as if you were there with her? Explain.

Write your answer in continuous prose.

Check your answer

1 When you have completed your answer to the example question:
   a) check that you have satisfied all the assessment objectives for
      reading (see page viii)
   b) look at the mark scheme for reading non-fiction texts on page x –
      which mark band do you think your answer is in? Explain why.
2 If your teacher marks your answer, consider his or her comments and
   how your mark fits in the mark scheme. Which mark band is your
   answer in? Can you see why?
3 Consider what you could try to do to move into a higher mark band.

Practice 3

On this occasion you are given prompts to help you find your way to an answer and you are given possible responses to these prompts to compare with your own.

Example question

Read the extract below. It is adapted from Julian Barnes's *Something to Declare*. The author, who now loves nothing more than France and the French, recalls how he felt when his parents took him to France for the first time when he was a boy.

Write about:

* Julian Barnes's reactions to his first experiences of France and French life

(Assessment objectives i, ii, iv)

* how he uses language to entertain the reader. (Assessment objectives iv, v)

First Time Abroad

That first, monstrous expedition into the exotic was a gentle tour of Normandy. From Dieppe we drove to Cany-Barville, of which I remember only two things: a vast and watery soup pullulating with some non-British grain or pulse; and being sent out on my first foreign morning for the newspaper. Which one did they want? Oh, just get the local one my father replied unhelpfully. I had the normal adolescent's self-consciousness – that's to say one that weighs like a stone-filled rucksack and feels of a different order to everyone else's. It was a heroic journey across the street and towards the shop, imperilled at every step by garlic-chewing low-lifes who drank red wine for breakfast and cut their bread – and youngsters' throats – with pocket knives. '*Le journal de la région,*' I repeated mantrically to myself. '*Le journal de la région, le journal de la région.*' I no longer remember if I uttered the words, or just flung my coins down with a cry of 'Keep the change.' All I remember is the purity of my fear, the absoluteness of my embarrassment, and the lack of vivid praise from my parents on my safe return.

And then there was the formidable eccentricity of the food. Their butter was wanly unsalted, blood came out of their meat, and they would put anything, absolutely anything, into soup. They grew perfectly edible tomatoes and then doused them in foul vinaigrette; ditto lettuce, ditto carrots, ditto beetroot. Normally you could detect that foul vinaigrette had been slimed over the salad; but sometimes they fooled you by slurping it into the bottom of the bowl, so that when with hopeful heart you lifted a leaf from the top … Bread was good (but see butter); chips were good (but see meat); vegetables were unpredictable. What were those things that weren't proper runner beans but round, fat, overcooked, and – cold! There was pate: forget it, anything could have gone into that; though not as anything as the anything that went into their gristly, warty *saucissons*, assembled from the disposings of an axe murderer. There was cheese. No, there were thousands of cheeses, and I would eat only one of them – Gruyère. Fruit was reliable – not much they could do to ruin that; indeed,

they grew very large and juicy red apples you could positively look forward to. They liked onions far too much. They brushed their teeth with garlic paste. They camouflaged quite edible meat and fish with sauces of dubious origin and name. Then there was wine, which bore a close resemblance to vinaigrette; and coffee, which I hated. Occasionally there would be a noxious, unassessable dish which explained all too well what you found and smelt behind the teak-stained door of *les waters*, where gigantic feet in knobbled porcelain awaited you, followed by a gigantic flush which drenched your turn-ups.

There are two parts to the question:

- the first asks for basic *understanding* of the text
- the second is about the *language* used. The second part requires detailed, close reading and appreciation of the text; this is where the highest marks are.

Assessment objectives

The assessment objectives are given for each part of the question so you can see:

- why the question has been asked
- what the examiners are looking for in your answer.

Go back to page viii to remind yourself of the assessment objectives.

Examiners' advice

Remember that your first reading should be at your normal reading speed, without stopping to consider each point closely, picking up the general idea. Closer reading – looking for specific ways of answering the question – comes later. However, as you read for the first time try to identify the tone of the piece.

Activity 2.5

Focus on *tone*. Remember the definition on page 19.

With a partner, discuss the tone of this passage. In this case Julian Barnes is obviously trying to make us laugh. But who does he want us to laugh at? Think carefully before you answer.

Approaches to the first part of the question

Write about:

• Julian Barnes's reactions to his first experiences of France and French life

Examiners' advice

● When you come to write your answer to the question there is, of course, no need to deal with each part of the question separately. You may do so if you wish, but it is actually often easier to deal with them both at the same time. When you write about the content (first bullet point), it is very difficult to do so without referring to the language (second bullet point), and vice versa.

● However, as you read the passage for the second time, you should consider the content – what the piece is about – first.

PROMPTS

▶ Go through the passage noting exactly what the experiences were that he is describing.

▶ Make a note of his reactions to each of these experiences.

▶ Consider the tone of the young Julian Barnes's reactions as they are described.

▶ Consider how he wants his readers to respond to what he writes.

Possible responses

Here are some possible responses to the prompts above. Check them against what you found.

- Julian Barnes tells us first that he and his parents were touring in Normandy. He remembers the soup and the trip to the newsagent's shop to collect the local paper. He tells us about some of the people he saw. In the second paragraph he tells us much more about about the different kinds of food he encountered.

- The soup, Barnes tells us, was awful (more about food later), and the trip to the paper shop was terrifying. He recalls the dread felt by all of us – but by teenagers in particular – of being made to feel inadequate and stupid. He regarded the locals with horror and fled back to his parents who completely failed to understand what he had been going through. In the second paragraph he gives us graphic details of the food, virtually all of which he found inedible.

- The tone of the piece is unmistakable – he's trying to make us laugh. You might be forgiven for thinking that Barnes wants us to laugh at France and French people, but in reality, of course, he wants us to laugh at himself. Not only himself, perhaps, but British people in general – and this means you. He wants us to laugh at ourselves.

- Julian Barnes is recalling his first trip abroad. He arrived on the European mainland very suspicious and almost expecting the worst – as many white, Anglo-Saxon, middle-class British people like himself do! His observations about the food are entirely typically British, too (at least true of Brits of his generation) – if it's foreign it's potentially lethal!

- Most easily misunderstood are his deliberately exaggerated portraits of the first French people he encountered. They are not factually accurate, of course; they are comic, stereotypical caricatures – born of the young Julian Barnes's upbringing. Compared with today's generation, relatively few of Julian Barnes's parents' generation would ever have travelled abroad. Lack of contact with and ignorance of other cultures breed suspicion and fear. It is, of course, this very failing which Barnes wants us to laugh at – certainly not the French and their culture. If you mention this you will be showing evidence of assessment objective iii – the ability to distinguish fact from opinion.

Approaches to the second part of the question

The key to answering questions concerned with the analysis of language is to select examples which are appropriate. It is also useful to be able to use some technical terms.

Before you answer the second part of the question, check that you understand the following definitions and try the activities.

Definition

Hyperbole means exaggeration. Sometimes, to intensify our feelings, we deliberately use exaggeration in our writing.

Activity 2.6

Focus on technical terms: *hyperbole*.

1 Find one example of hyperbole in Julian Barnes's piece.
2 Use hyperbole to describe the worst meal *you* have ever tasted!

> **Definition**
>
> **Onomatopoeia** is the technique of using a word which actually sounds like the action it describes, for example, *snap, crackle and pop*.

Activity 2.7

Focus on technical terms: *onomatopoeia*.

1 Use onomatopoeia to describe the sound made by your stomach after the worst meal you have ever tasted!
2 Find the onomatopoeic word used in Barnes's second paragraph to describe the sound of soup being poured into his bowl.

Now answer the second part of the example question:

Write about:

• how he uses language to entertain the reader.

Examiners' advice

When you are reading the passage for the third time, you need to do so more slowly, noting specific examples of how the writer has used language for different purposes and effects. You will not be able to write about all of these in the examination, because there simply isn't enough time, so you have to be selective, picking out the most striking – in this case entertaining – examples. Demonstrating a knowledge of some technical terms will also impress the examiner.

PROMPTS

The first paragraph

▶ Which two words in the opening sentence lead us to anticipate that all did not go well on this trip?
▶ How does the writer make eating soup appear to be a daunting prospect?
▶ What simile is used to describe teenage self-consciousness?

▶ What device is the writer using when he describes his trip to the shop as an 'heroic journey'?
▶ What is Barnes trying to do when he describes his encounters with 'garlic-chewing low-lifes'?

continued

PROMPTS *continued*

The second paragraph

▶ What do you make of the phrase 'formidable eccentricity', used to describe French food?
▶ What onomatopoeic words does Barnes use to describe eating?
▶ What other words are used to tell us how disgusting he found the food?
▶ Find examples of hyperbole used by Barnes in the second paragraph and explain why you think he has used them.

Possible responses

Here are some possible responses to the prompts above. Check them against what you found.

First paragraph

● The trip was clearly intended to be 'gentle' but turned out to be 'monstrous' – the juxtaposition (putting together) of these two conflicting adjectives is amusing in itself, and the exaggeration (hyperbole) in 'monstrous' leads us to anticipate a series of equally exaggerated anecdotes to illustrate his point.

● Julian Barnes meets French (= potentially lethal) food for the first time. The soup is described as 'vast' and 'pullulating'. Few readers are likely to understand the meaning of the second of these adjectives – 'pullulating' here means 'teeming' or 'overflowing', suggesting, with 'vast', that the bowl is massive and unending, like the ocean. But the word is almost onomatopoeic, too; as your mouth forms the syllables you can almost hear the sounds of bubbles bursting on the surface. Some might even think of the sound of vomiting!

● Hyperbole is being used once again, as it is throughout the passage. It is, in fact, the most obvious source of the humour in the passage as Barnes recalls the enormity of his first impressions. In Julian Barnes's young eyes his walk across the road was just as dangerous as Scott's trip to the Antarctic or Ulysses's Odyssey.

● When he describes such a trivial trip as an 'heroic journey' he is mocking himself.

● Not for one minute does Julian Barnes

actually believe that Frenchmen are as he describes them here. These pictures are caricatures, exaggerating features which the writer in his naiveté and ignorance feared most. English food when Barnes was a boy was infamously bland whereas the French were thought to be more adventurous in their use of strong-tasting foods such as garlic. Hence the fear of these strange, exotic people is depicted in the phrase 'garlic-chewing'. The same idea is repeated in 'who drank red wine for breakfast' highlighting supposed differences between the French and the English – all of whom are supposed to drink good, wholesome beer.

● As for the ludicrous picture of Frenchmen slitting 'youngsters' throats', this is taken straight from the fairy stories read to him as a child. As a little boy he was terrified of ogres and monsters in these stories and he transfers these fears onto a people he simply fails to understand.

Second paragraph

● Here the writer uses a similar technique, exaggerating the differences in culture between the English and French and the consequent fear that many English people had, and some still have, of the French. He focuses on food and tells us how he simply couldn't come to terms with it. The pompous phrase 'formidable eccentricity' prepares us for more exaggeration. ('Formidable', incidentally, is a frequently used word in French when expressing admiration!) Words such as 'doused' and

continued on page 68

continued from page 67

'foul' (repeated) are used, as are 'slimed', 'slurping', 'gristly', 'warty' and 'noxious' to capture how offensive to all of his senses these things were. The humour once again lies in the fact that the writer is laughing at himself and at any of his countrymen who, in their ignorance, might still be prejudiced. He, of course, as he has grown more accustomed to it, has discovered the truth about French food – that it is delicious – and in this passage is poking fun at those of us who remain less enlightened about other cultures and traditions.

- Very funny phrases such as 'the disposings of an axe murderer' and 'they brushed their teeth with garlic paste' remind us of what Barnes was up to in the first paragraph.
- Perhaps the most distasteful picture, however, is when he writes about the lavatory to which the 'foul vinaigrette' inevitably drives him. The English middle-classes are renowned in many other countries for being the most prudish people in the world. Some subjects are simply not spoken about – especially lavatories. Julian Barnes's parents, therefore, would almost certainly have not prepared him for the 'gigantic' (repeated) shock of walking into a French lavatory – very different in those days from the ones usually found in England. (To understand exactly how funny this picture is you might have to do a little research – ask your teachers or your parents, who might be familiar with *les waters*.)

When you are ready to do so, select material from your notes and ideas from any discussion and write your answer in continuous prose. Remember, you cannot possibly include anything like all of the above (this is merely to identify the kinds of things the examiner is looking for).

Check your answer

1 When you have completed your answer to the example question:
 a) check that you have satisfied all the assessment objectives for reading (see page viii)
 b) look at the mark scheme for reading non-fiction texts on page x – which mark band do you think your answer is in? Explain why.
2 If your teacher marks your answer, consider his or her comments and how your mark fits in the mark scheme. Which mark band is your answer in? Can you see why?
3 Consider what you could try to do to move into a higher mark band.

Practice 4

Remember that on this occasion, although you will be given prompts to help you, you will have to find the answers for yourself.

Example question

Read the extract below. It comes from Alan Bennett's book *Writing Home*. In this extract he recalls his childhood in Leeds during the Second World War.

Write about:

- the differences between real life as described in textbooks and real life as experienced by Bennett himself   (Assessment objectives i, ii, iii, iv)

- how the writer uses language to express his disappointment with life as he finds it.   (Assessment objectives iv, v)

Fact or Fiction

Had it been only stories that didn't measure up to the world it wouldn't have been so bad. But it wasn't only fiction that was fiction. Fact too was fiction, as textbooks seemed to bear no more relation to the real world than did the story-books. At school or in my *Boy's Book of the Universe* I read of the minor wonders of nature – the sticklebacks that haunted the most ordinary pond, the newts and toads said to lurk under every stone, and the dragonflies that flitted over the dappled surface. Not, so far as I could see, in Leeds. There were owls in hollow trees, so the nature books said, but I saw no owls – and hollow trees were in pretty short supply too. The only department where nature actually lined up with the text was frog-spawn. Even in Leeds there was that, jamjars of which I dutifully fetched home to stand beside great wilting bunches of bluebells on the backyard window-sill. But the tadpoles never seemed to graduate to the full-blown frogs the literature predicted, invariably giving up the ghost as soon as they reached the two-legged stage when, unbeknownst to Mam, they would have to be flushed secretly down the lav.

It was the same when we went on holiday. If the books were to be believed, every seashore was littered with starfish and delicately whorled shells, seahorses in every rockpool and crabs the like of which I had seen only in Macfisheries' window. Certainly I never came across them at Morecambe, nor any of the other advertised treasures of the seashore. There was only a vast, untenanted stretch of mud and somewhere beyond it the sea, invisible, unpaddleable and strewn with rolls of barbed wire to discourage any parachutist undiscerning enough to choose to land there.

These evidences of war and general shortage of treats and toys made me somehow blame the shortcomings of the natural world on the current hostilities. I don't recall

continued on page 70

continued from page 69

seeing a single magnolia tree in blossom until I was fifteen or so, and when I did I found myself thinking 'Well, they probably didn't have them during the war.' And so it was with shells and starfish and the rest of Nature's delights; she had put these small treasures into storage for the duration, along with signposts, neon lights and the slot machines for Five Boys chocolate that stood, invariably empty, on every railway platform.

There are two parts to the question:

- the first asks for basic *understanding* of the text
- the second is about the *language* used. The second part requires detailed, close reading and appreciation of the text; this is where the highest marks are.

Assessment objectives

The assessment objectives are given for each part of the question so you can see:

- why the question has been asked
- what the examiners are looking for in your answer.

Go back to page viii to remind yourself of the assessment objectives.

Examiners' advice

- Again, it is very likely that you will write about both parts of the question together – your comments about content will include references to the language and vice-versa – but as you are preparing to write it is a good idea to consider each part in turn.
- Begin, as always, by reading the passage at your normal reading speed – to gain a general idea of the content and the tone the writer is using – without pausing to consider any point in detail.
- How would you describe the tone? Is it happy or sad? As Bennett looks back at his childhood is he angry or amused? Could it possibly be several of these at the same time? Could he have, as we say, mixed feelings?

Approaches to the first part of the question

Write about:

- the differences between real life as described in textbooks and real life as experienced by Bennett himself

PROMPTS

- ► What does Alan Bennett read about 'real life' in his textbooks?
- ► What does he find for himself in Leeds and when he goes on holiday?
- ► How are these two versions of real life different from each other?

- ► How does Alan Bennett react to the differences he feels exist between the two versions of reality he describes?
- ► What response is he looking for from his readers?

Approaches to the second part of the question

Write about:

- how the writer uses language to express his disappointment with life as he finds it.

Examiners' advice

As you read the passage for the final time, make a list of the words and phrases Bennett uses to describe his attitude towards the world as described in textbooks and of those used to describe his attitude to the world as he actually found it. Consider the significance of the differences between them.

PROMPTS

- Why, when referring to the textbooks, does he refer to 'minor wonders of nature'?
- Comment on the sense of mystery in phrases like 'sticklebacks ... haunted' and 'newts and toads ... lurk', and 'dragonflies ... flitted'.
- What is the significance of the fact that the bluebells are 'wilting'?
- How do you feel when you read about frog-spawn being 'flushed down the lav'?
- What do you make of 'littered with starfish' and 'delicately whorled shells'?

- Why 'treasures of the sea shore'?
- What is the effect on the reader of describing Morecambe beach as 'vast and untenanted'?
- How do you feel when you are told the sea was 'unpaddleable' during the war years?
- Why does the writer personify (turn into a person) Nature in the final paragraph?
- Why 'delights' and 'treasures' (repeated)?

When you are ready, write your answer to the question in continuous prose.

Check your answer

1 When you have completed your answer to the example question:
   a) check that you have satisfied all the assessment objectives for reading (see page viii)
   b) look at the mark scheme for reading non-fiction texts on page x – which mark band do you think your answer is in? Explain why.
2 If your teacher marks your answer, consider his or her comments and how your mark fits in the mark scheme. Which mark band is your answer in? Can you see why?
3 Consider what you could try to do to move into a higher mark band.

Practice 5

The question in this section appears just as it will on the examination paper – completely without prompts. You are on your own.

Specimen examination question

Paper 1, Section B: Non-fiction texts

Question 2

Read the following passage. It is an extract from *A Mad World My Masters* by John Simpson, the BBC World Affairs Editor. In this piece he describes his first meeting with Diana, Princess of Wales.

- Explain John Simpson's attitude towards the way in which society and the media treated the Princess of Wales and how he felt when he met her for the first time.

- How does the writer use language to impress his feelings upon us?

The Princess

Royal reporting isn't my thing, and like a great many people I thought the hounding of Diana by the tabloid press was one of the most disgusting spectacles of modern times. And yet the defence the tabloids put forward – that she sought out the publicity – was certainly true; though it would be more accurate to say that she craved attention, not the destructive and unjustifiable prying which the tabloids went in for.

Their money lured her friends and associates (and the unspeakable people such as those who recorded her private telephone conversations and those of her husband) into betraying her. Diana was not a saint; hers was a complicated and quite fragile personality, which could not stand the strain of so much savage interference. The way the tabloids smacked their lips over the most intimate details of her personal life shamed our entire society; and sometimes journalists seemed to be the only people who did not understand this.

I first met Diana in 1989, at a state banquet at Buckingham Palace for the President of Nigeria. It was a superb occasion, and when the lights went down and a lone piper strode along the corridor leading to the hall, accompanying the waiters in full livery who were bringing in the pudding, there was an audible and delighted intake of breath all around me. They do things the old-fashioned way at Buckingham Palace. After dinner, the ordinary guests stood around in one drawing room drinking coffee, while the royal family and the guests of honour stood in the adjoining one. There was no physical barrier between the two rooms, yet no one crossed the *cordon sanitaire* without invitation.

continued on page 74

continued from page 73

I had just come back from a fairly high-profile trip to Ceausescu's Romania, where I had been arrested several times. One of the royal dukes wanted to talk about all this, and once across the magic line I stayed there, chatting to other people as well. When the conversation finally ran out I stood slightly irresolute and wondering whether I should leave. Then a low, half-familiar voice spoke behind me.

'I've been looking forward all night to meeting you.'

The words carried an extraordinary attraction. I turned, and saw Diana standing there in a low-cut white dress with diamonds around her neck and in her hair. I was of course mesmerised. I suppose that was the point of the whole thing. It didn't matter to me that she must have used the same line hundreds of times before, and probably several times that evening.

We talked for half an hour, while the waiters went round with trays of superb brandy. I didn't need the brandy. Did she mind, I asked, if I didn't call her 'Your Royal Highness'? She didn't. She told me about her life, and about the way the tabloids made her life a misery.

'If you ever need any help in that department,' I said, 'just let me know.' I didn't know exactly what I meant by that, but I was definitely in knight-errant mood.

'Thank you,' she said. 'I won't forget it.'

Not long afterwards the Prince of Wales came over, and after a few more words they walked away together.

'It was wonderful to meet you,' Diana murmured.

There are few things more susceptible than the heart of a man in early middle-age, and I was completely bowled over. Plenty of others must have had precisely the same experience. It was too late to find a taxi, and I walked home to South Kensington in my rented white tie and tails without noticing the cold, the distance or the stares of occasional passers-by.

Check your answer

1 When you have completed your answer to the specimen question:
   a) check that you have satisfied all the assessment objectives for reading (see page viii)
   b) look at the mark scheme for reading non-fiction texts on page x – which mark band do you think your answer is in? Explain why.
2 If your teacher marks your answer, consider his or her comments and how your mark fits in the mark scheme. Which mark band is your answer in? Can you see why?
3 Consider what you could try to do to move into a higher mark band.

Section B

Section B is a test of writing. You are advised to take 40 minutes to answer the question in Section B and it is worth 15 per cent of the final mark, the same as for Section A (see the mark scheme for writing on page xi). This writing question is therefore as valuable to you as the reading questions and is proportionately very important.

For GCSE English you have to show your ability to write in four different ways:

- to explore, imagine, entertain) you will do this as coursework
- to inform, explain, describe)
- to argue, persuade, advise – Paper 1, Section B, see Chapter 3
- to analyse, review, comment – Paper 2, Section B, see Chapter 5.

The question in Section B will relate to the assessment objectives for writing, which are set out on page viii.

3 Writing to argue, persuade, advise

The question you are set in the examination may include all or some of these purposes – to argue, to persuade, to advise. Check that you understand the following definitions and try the activities.

Definitions

- **Argue** If your purpose is to argue, you will need to have a clearly defined point of view, evidence to support it and some general, wider considerations to present on the topic.
- **Persuade** If your purpose is to persuade, you will need to present facts and opinions which will change somebody else's point of view, or change their actions or get them to do something.
- **Advise** If your aim is to advise, you will offer evidence about what will happen in certain circumstances and make a recommendation for people to act upon.

Activity 3.1

Write clearly in one sentence your view on fox hunting and what you think the government should do about it. Make a list of strong words you might use in your essay. Here are some to start you off.

If you were *against* fox hunting, for example:

    cruel
    murderous
    unfair.

If you were *for* fox hunting, for example:

    pest
    vermin
    innocent chickens and lambs.

Use a thesaurus. Collect words from other people.

Activity 3.2

You think smoking is a bad habit. Write the opening line of a letter to a friend who has just started smoking.

Make a list of persuasive words you might include in your letter. Here are some to start you off:

bad breath
uncool
life expectancy
more sense.

Use a thesaurus. Collect words from other people.

The question you are likely to be set in the examination will almost certainly combine some of these aspects. For example, a question might look like this:

An article you have read in a newspaper recently states that people are spending money they don't really have and saving nothing for the future.

Write an article in reply which argues for or against the idea that people should be made by law to save for their retirement.

The question states the context of the topic, and the audience (i.e. people who may not save enough of their income) and asks you to argue for or against a specific idea. It should also be clear that if your argument is a good one you will be advising people what to do. This question is an argue/advise question. You can answer this question in *Practice 5* on page 101.

Here is another example:

There have been a number of traffic accidents and near misses recently on a main road in a residential area near you which have involved children.

Write a letter to your council highways department which tries to persuade them that a pedestrian crossing with traffic lights is essential.

The question states the context of the topic, and the audience (i.e. the highways department) and asks you to persuade somebody specific to do something. It is also clear that the action is advisable because it will save lives. This question is a persuade/advise question. You can answer this question in *Practice 7* on page 102.

A question might easily contain all of the elements mentioned above. If you consider the question carefully and think about the purpose and audience then you will cover them all.

The purposes – argue, persuade, advise – are connected or might be said to be similar in intention; hopefully you can see that. But they are subtly different too.

In this chapter practice is provided by analysing four modelled pieces of writing, followed by three specimen examination questions:

- Writing to argue, advise
  Practice 1, page 80 – modelled writing 'Green electricity', with prompts and sample responses
  Practice 2, page 87 – modelled writing 'Why football may stay at home', with prompts
- Writing to persuade, advise
  Practice 3, page 92 – modelled writing 'Food for life', with prompts and sample responses
  Practice 4, page 97 – modelled writing 'The Shetland Islands', with prompts
- Practice 5–7, pages 101–2 – specimen examination questions, exactly like the examination – you are given no help at all.

Writing to argue, advise

If the purpose of your writing is to argue, your writing will need to show the following aspects:

- a clearly defined point of view, a clear aim, a focus of attention, a topic which is unambiguous: you will be given the topic in the question and you need to make it clear that you understand it
- evidence to support your point of view which may be facts, feelings and opinions based on **anecdotal** evidence, experience or expert opinion; you may quote experts which you make up yourself
- alternatives to what you are arguing in order to refute them (prove them wrong) and set them aside
- general, wider considerations, for example of a moral, economic, social or even political dimension.

You will also need to:

- show awareness of your audience
- use words and phrases effectively.

> **Definition**
>
> An **anecdote** is a story used to illustrate a point.

Before you start, remind yourself of the following definitions and activities:

- audience, page 17, Activity 1.12
- the effective use of language, page 15, Activities 1.9, 1.10, 1.11
- fact and opinion, page 10, Activities 1.4, 1.5, 1.15, 1.16
- argument, page 11, Activity 1.6

and the assessment objectives for writing on page viii.

Practice 1

Modelled writing: argue, advise

Read the article below, which is from the People & Planet website.

Then work through the prompts which follow the article. Finding the answers to these prompts will teach you why and how the article is a successful argument. On this occasion, you are given some possible responses.

People & the Planet

Today every University in Britain could be buying green electricity.

So why aren't they?

Climate change is happening now.

It's caused by greenhouse gases released by burning oil, coal and gas, mainly to produce electricity.

*   **Fact:** The ten warmest years ever measured worldwide have all occurred since 1981. 1998 was the warmest of the previous 1000 years.
*   **Fact:** During the 1960s there were 16 climate-related natural disasters. During the 1990s there were 70.
*   **Fact:** By 2025 over half of all people living in developing countries, will be 'highly vulnerable' to floods and storms.

Big electricity users like Universities must switch to green electricity.

Wealthy nations like Britain produce 80% of greenhouse gases, risking the lives and livelihoods of one billion people who are threatened by the effects of climate change.

To help stop climate change Universities must cut their greenhouse gas emissions substantially. Switching to green electricity, generated from solar, wind or wave power, is the only way for Universities to do this.

It's easy for Universities to switch and it won't cost much extra. In fact, of the three UK Universities that already use green electricity, in two cases it hasn't cost them a penny more! ...

Last year, UK Institutes of Higher Education consumed around 0.5% of all electricity generated in the UK.

As major electricity consumers, Universities have a clear responsibility to rapidly reduce their emissions of greenhouse gases to help prevent further climatic destabilisation. As the required 60–70% reductions will not be achieved by energy conservation measures alone, switching to 'green' electricity, which does not

continued

continued

contribute to climate change, is the only way for Universities to meet this responsibility.

Since 1998 it has been possible to purchase 'green' electricity generated from renewable power sources (e.g. wind, wave, solar, etc.) and it is now widely available from major electricity supply companies.

Although green electricity may be expected to be between zero and 10% more expensive than conventional supplies, two University case studies in this report indicate that economically-neutral supply contracts are possible. ...

Furthermore, in practical terms, switching should be a simple task, involving only the negotiation of a new supply contract.

Whilst it may make economic sense to switch to green electricity, this should not overshadow the moral imperative to act. It should not be forgotten that although industrialised countries like the UK are causing climate change, it is mainly the world's poor who are paying the price. Climate-related natural disasters are increasing in frequency and 96% of deaths from such disasters occur in developing countries.

People & Planet is therefore calling on every University in the UK to:

- **immediately obtain quotations for the supply of green electricity**
- **make a public commitment to switch the University to a 100% green electricity supply as soon as is practically possible, and certainly within three years.**

adapted from www.peopleandplanet.org/climatechange/greenelectricity

Examiners' advice

If you can find an answer to each of the following prompts you will have understood the aspects referred to on page 79, *Writing to argue, advise*. Remind yourself of these.

PROMPTS

Look at the title and sub-title and the way in which they are written.

▶ What is the writer's topic? Has she stated the topic clearly?

▶ Where and how has she done this?

▶ How has the writer involved the reader from the very beginning?

Look at the first three paragraphs and the statistics they include.

▶ Where does the writer state her point of view clearly?

▶ What is the purpose of presenting the three 'facts'?

▶ How does the writer show that she understands the topic?

▶ How does the writer show she is quite clear in her point of view?

▶ What is the persuasive point made to support the argument in the last of these paragraphs? How does this work? Who is it aimed at?

continued on page 82

PROMPTS *continued*

Read the next four paragraphs, from 'Last year ...' to '... new supply contract'.

▶ How does the writer develop the argument in this section?

▶ What are the types of evidence being called upon here? Which are facts, which are opinions and which are speculation?

▶ Does the writer use 'expert' opinion or science to support her views?

▶ Is there any way we can know if the facts and figures are true?

▶ Does this matter to the strength of the argument?

Look back on the article so far.

▶ Has the writer dealt with the alternatives to green electricity in order to refute (disprove) them and set them aside?

▶ How and where has she done this?

Does the writer make a general, moral point to support the argument?

▶ What is the moral point, in your own words?

▶ Who is this moral point aimed at?

▶ Is it likely to be an effective argument? Why?

Look at the conclusion to the article, both the words and the layout.

▶ What is the writer demanding?

▶ Is this a strong or a weak conclusion? Why?

The power of the words you use will affect the power of your argument.

Find and list some words and phrases from the text which are vivid or particularly effective. State briefly why they are so.

Possible responses

Here are some possible responses to the prompts above. Check them against what you found.

Title and sub-title

● The writer has stated the topic in the title and expanded it in the sub-title. She uses the phrase 'green electricity' cleverly since it is a metaphor (remember the definition on page 22), is intended to entice people into an explanation and draw them into the argument. She also focuses the reader to 'every university in Britain', which is the target audience for action.

● The reader is involved because the writer uses a rhetorical question in the title. It tells the reader that the universities are not doing what they should. It seems to be asking the reader a question, but in fact it is an invitation to read on.

First three paragraphs

● The writer states her point of view early in the article and repeats it. She writes, 'Big electricity users like Universities must switch to green electricity', and later, 'To help stop climate change Universities must cut their greenhouse gas emissions...'. The writer emphasises her point in this way.

● The writer gives credibility and strength to her argument with facts. They are easy to read and understand. They show she has knowledge to support her point of view. She shows that things are getting worse and uses dramatic phrases and large figures to keep the reader's attention. Her understanding of the topic is supported by research. She uses the word 'must' twice and 'substantially' to show she is clear about the argument — there is no choice.

● The writer states that it is 'easy' to do what is being suggested. She pre-empts (anticipates) arguments about cost. This

continued

continued

is persuasive because it removes a major argument against.

● *It is skilful to anticipate and remove arguments against your point of view.*

Next four paragraphs

● This is a development section and all good argument essays must have one. This is where the writer consolidates (builds on) the argument, the tone is less dramatic and reason and observation are used.

● The writer appeals to a sense of responsibility, offers information and reinforces the need for green electricity to meet targets. The writer is honest about the cost but reassuring as well. It is obviously a matter of opinion that green electricity will do all the things claimed for it, but the opinion is offered as fact.

● The tone of this section is reasonable, but persuasive, almost seductive, finally explaining how easy it would be to accept the writer's argument and adopt her suggestions.

● Notice that the writer does not give up on her main, clear mission (purpose). She states, 'Universities have a clear responsibility …' and 'The only way for Universities to meet this …'.

● It is not always possible for the average reader to check scientific 'facts' or experts' opinions. This does not matter. *In your 'argument' essays in the exam you can make up facts and invent experts. As long as they are clever enough to seem real, they will strengthen your argument.*

● The writer states clearly at the beginning of the article that climate change is caused by burning oil, coal and gas. The opposition to her argument is kept in the forefront as a target to be attacked. Sometimes the opposition is called 'greenhouse gases', sometimes 'emissions', sometimes' conventional supplies'. *An important way of supporting your argument is to destroy or attack the opposition.*

The article so far

● The writer states a general, moral point towards the end of the argument, '… this should not overshadow the moral imperative to act'.

● She then goes on to develop the point that the 'world's poor' are suffering because of greenhouse emissions.

The writer's general moral point

● In this article this is aimed at the intelligent reader with a conscience. People who work in, or make decisions in, universities might be persuaded by a moral argument. In fact most people might.

● *In order to achieve higher marks in writing an argument, you need to make a general, moral argument as well as a factual one.*

The conclusion

● The conclusion sums up the argument, recalls the topic and, in this case, calls for some action. Here some demands are being made because the tone of the argument is strong. The writer goes beyond advising the universities – she's telling them to 'obtain quotations' and 'make a public commitment'. You could say it was strong advice.

● This is a strong conclusion, rounded and effective. The reader is in no doubt about the writer's point of view. She has also used layout for effective emphasis.

The power of words

● The writer has written this article in a very straightforward and easy to understand way. But there are a number of powerful and effective words and phrases which are worth noting, for example, 'climate-related natural disasters', 'highly vulnerable', 'risking the lives and livelihoods', 'rapidly reduce', 'climatic destabilisation', 'moral imperative'.

● *The more interesting and extended your vocabulary in your writing, the more marks you will be awarded.*

To help you understand better the assessment objectives for writing, check that you understand the following definitions and advice, and try the activities, which are based on the article you have just read.

Definitions

'communicate *clearly* and *imaginatively*'

- **Clearly** means that you should avoid confusing your reader.
- **Imaginatively** means you need to keep your audience interested in what you are writing.

Examiners' advice

- Put yourself in the position of the reader in order to check that what you are writing is *clear*. The direction of your argument must be obvious and unambiguous. You should not cloud your argument with too many facts and examples. You are taking the readers on a journey – make sure they get there.
- Your writing should be *imaginative* when writing an argument in that it keeps the reader interested. Give the reader some pictures for his or her mind. 'Green' electricity is a picture.

Activity 3.3

1. In a simple sentence, write down the main point the writer wants to get across in the article about green electricity
2. Find some more pictures in the article.

Definitions

'use and adapt forms for *different readers and purposes*'

To do this you need to think about your audience (see page 17) and the register you use (see below).

Register refers to the different ways we speak or write to different kinds of people. You may write in a very formal way, or in a very elaborate, descriptive way, or sometimes your writing may be chatty, informal, more like everyday spoken language. The use of slang and colloquialism is part of register, as is dialect. Consider, for example, the way you speak to your friends at school and the way you speak to your grandparents.

Examiners' advice

- You must decide and be clear about who your *audience* is. Sometimes it is straightforward. In the first example given on page 78, you are being asked to write to the readers of a newspaper about a specific topic, so they are your audience. If you write a letter to a newspaper about the amount of litter on your street you may have a number of potential audiences: the editor, the general readership, people who drop litter or the council who are not picking it up. You must decide who your audience is.

● You must select an appropriate *register* when writing. Since you are expected to write in standard English, chatty, slang, loosely constructed register is less likely to be appropriate.

● Here are some words which describe register: informative, factual, emotive, formal, technical, ceremonial, casual, intimate, social, commercial, political, jargon, slang, colloquial, combative, arcane, esoteric.

Activity 3.4

Explain who the audience is for the article on green electricity. Is this made clear? How?

Activity 3.5

1   Which words would you use to describe the register of the article about green electricity?

2   Does the writer use a number of different registers?

Definitions

'Organise ideas ... using a variety of *linguistic* and *structural features*'

● **Linguistic features/devices** – see the definition on page 18.

● **Structural features/devices** These are the different ways the writing can be put together (constructed) for different purposes/audiences, for example, using different length paragraphs for effect, different length sentences for emphasis or information, indentation, bullet points, bold type face and effective headings and sub-headings. The overall shape of the writing, how and where ideas are presented and developed is also a structural device. The main argument or point of view may not, for example, be at the beginning.

Examiners' advice

You should employ linguistic and structural techniques in your writing. But remember not to overdo them. Make sure they are appropriate for your audience and purpose.

Activity 3.6

The writer of the article on green electricity could have employed the rhetorical question in her piece. For example, instead of writing:

'Wealthy nations like Britain produce 80% of greenhouse gases, risking the lives and livelihoods of one billion people who are threatened by the effects of climate change.'

she might have written:

'Wealthy nations like Britain produce 80% of greenhouse gases. Do we really want to go on risking the lives and livelihoods of one billion people who are threatened by the effects of climate change?'

Change the following statement into a rhetorical question:

'Universities have an obligation to cut their emission of greenhouse gasses.'

Activity 3.7

1   Find examples of the use of rhetorical devices in the article on green electricity.
2   Make some changes of your own, like the one above. Is the effect better or not?

Activity 3.8

1   Find and describe the structural devices used in the article on green electricity.
2   Produce a structure plan for a leaflet arguing against fox hunting. On a blank piece of paper, draw rectangles for paragraphs, bullet points, lines for title and paragraph titles, etc.

Assessment objectives check

Although this article was, of course, not written for a GCSE examination, are you satisfied that it:

● communicates clearly and imaginatively? (Assessment objective i)
● organises ideas into sentences, paragraphs and a whole text using a variety of linguistic and structural features? (Assessment objective ii)
● uses a range of sentence structures effectively with accurate punctuation and spelling? (Assessment objective iii)
● successfully argues in favour of green electricity?
● advises a clear course of action?

Remind yourself of the definitions on page 77.

If so, then it is a successful piece in terms of argue, advise.

Practice 2

Modelled writing: argue/advise

Read the article 'Why football may stay at home' below. Then work through the prompts which follow. Finding the answers to these prompts will teach you why and how the article is a successful argument.

This time no sample responses are given – you will have to find the answers on your own, or in a pair or group discussion.

Why football may stay at home

Vivek Chaudhary argues that the capital may still be the best venue

If the government and the Football Association had paid a little more attention three years ago they would saved themselves a lot of embarrassment and a lot of expense.

As a ministerial working group gets underway today on how to salvage the farce that is the Wembley project, all the indications are that the country is going to end up with a national stadium close to the plans originally submitted around three years ago.

The FA, government and Sport England feel tied to Wembley. While there may be a number of options outside the capital, which have better transport facilities and lower construction costs, Wembley has emerged as the place where the national stadium must be constructed.

The message coming from those involved in the project is loud and clear – if it is going to be built then it has to be Wembley.

There are a number of advantages to keeping the national stadium at Wembley, the most important among them a financial one. If the stadium stays in north-west London then £120m of lottery money given to the FA to buy the Wembley site would not have to be paid back. This would save a lot of administrative hassle and arguing, which is likely to take place given that all the money has been spent.

Officials involved in the Wembley project believe that it is the best location in the country, despite constant criticism from those who attend matches there.

When invitations were first invited from English cities for the national stadium's location, Birmingham followed by Manchester was considered to have the best site. However, Sport England was soon informed by transport specialists that there would be severe congestion on motorways around the city with the M6 and M42 clogged for several hours after matches.

continued on page 88

continued from page 87

Wembley does not have the same problems. It is well serviced by a number of rail and tube stations and despite complaints, football fans can get away relatively easy.

Congestion on the motorways is also a problem with Birmingham's current attempt to become the national stadium's new home.

Manchester is the second favourite city to host the national stadium. However, it is felt that the stadium currently being constructed for next year's Commonwealth Games in the city is not big enough for a national stadium.

The Wembley area is one of the poorest in the country and both Brent council and central government are keen to ensure that the national stadium is con-structed there as a way of sparking economic regeneration. According to the local authority, around 20,000 jobs depend on the stadium being built and that not locating it at Wembley would cost the area an estimated £170m.

A Wembley official said: "We all know that the stadium comes in for a lot of criticism but the location of a new national stadium has been carefully thought out. We examined a lot of research. Wembley might not be the best place for a massive stadium but it's miles ahead of the others."

The feeling is that the entire project has been delayed enough and that starting from scratch at a new location is something that the project just cannot afford.

The Guardian

PROMPTS

Look at the title and sub-title.

▶ What are the various meanings and connected ideas associated with the words of the title?

▶ What does the sub-title tell you?

▶ How has the writer involved his readers from the beginning?

Read the first four paragraphs.

▶ Where is the main point made? Quote the words which state the argument.

▶ How does the writer introduce the alternatives to his view?

▶ Why does he do it here, however briefly?

▶ Which authorities and bodies does he mention and for what purpose? Is the writer arguing on behalf of others? Explain.

▶ How do we know his view on the matter?

▶ Comment on these phrases: 'paid a little more attention', 'salvage the farce', 'must be', 'loud and clear', 'it has to be'.

▶ What is the purpose emerging from the article at this point?

▶ Who are the writer's audience? Is there more than one?

▶ Make a comment on the register used by the writer.

Read the next two paragraphs, from 'There are a number of ...' to '... who attend matches there.'

▶ How does the writer develop the argument in this section?

▶ What are some of the key words?

▶ What evidence is there of colloquialism (informal language) so far in the article? What does this tell you about the writer's view of his audience?

Read the next four paragraphs, down to '... enough for a national stadium.'

▶ Has the writer dealt with alternatives to the position he evidently supports?

▶ Explain how he sets them out, then how he shows that they would not work.

▶ Do his arguments convince you?

Look back at the piece of writing so far.

▶ Is there a clear shape to the writing? Explain.

▶ Has the writer kept his audience with him throughout, so far?

Now read the third to last paragraph.

▶ What is the moral point being made?

▶ Why is this a clever move on the part of the writer?

▶ How does the writer reinforce this moral point?

Look at the concluding paragraph.

▶ What device does the writer use here?

▶ How is it constructed? Is it effective?

▶ How does the writer link his last idea in the piece of writing with his first?

Activity 3.9

Look back at the activities on page 84–6 to help you answer these questions.

1 Comment on the clarity of the article and the extent to which it has communicated ideas and developed them.

2 a) Explain who the audience is for the article.

   b) Is the audience kept in mind throughout? How?

3 a) Which words would you use to describe the register of the
       article?
   b) Is there more than one register employed by the writer? Explain.
   c) Are the registers appropriate?
4 a) Find examples of the use of linguistic or rhetorical devices in the
       article.
   b) Make some changes of your own and see whether the effect is
       better or not.
5 a) Find and comment on a number of the structural devices noted
       in the article.
   b) How do they enhance or strengthen the article?

Assessment objectives check

Although this article was, of course, not written for a GCSE examination,
are you satisfied that it:

- communicates clearly and imaginatively? (Assessment objective i)
- organises ideas into sentences, paragraphs and a whole text using a
  variety of linguistic and structural features? (Assessment objective ii)
- uses a range of sentence structures effectively with accurate
  punctuation and spelling? (Assessment objective iii)
- successfully argues in favour of football staying at Wembley?
- advises a clear course of action?

Remind yourself of the definitions on page 77.

If so, then it is a successful piece in terms of argue, advise.

Writing to persuade, advise

If the purpose is to persuade, your writing will need to show the
following aspects:

- a clearly defined view, opinion, focus and understanding of the issue.
  The topic will be given to you in the exam and will always be
  something about which you will have general knowledge and which
  probably links to the materials used for the reading questions
- evidence to support your point of view which may be facts, feelings
  and opinions based on anecdotal evidence, experience or expert
  opinion, you may quote experts which you make up yourself – as in
  the case of writing an argument. But now you must try to change
  people's behaviour, attitude or beliefs
- alternatives actions or beliefs to those you are urging in order to
  refute (disprove) them and set them aside
- general, wider considerations, for example, of a moral, economic,
  social or even political dimension.

You will also need to:

- show awareness of your audience
- use words and phrases effectively.

Before you go on to *Practice 3*, remind yourself of the following definitions and activities:

- audience, page 17, Activity 1.12
- the effective use of language, page 15, Activities 1.9, 1.10, 1.11
- fact and opinion, page 10, Activities 1.4, 1.5, 1.15, 1.16
- argument, page 11, Activity 1.6
- persuade, page 77

and the assessment objectives for writing on page viii.

Examiners' advice

Remember that there is a difference between arguing and persuading:

- You can argue your point of view and actually agree to differ, although in most arguments you would want to convince your opponent so that he or she agrees with you. But you can argue from your side only and leave it at that.
- But when you are persuading, what the other person ends up doing or thinking is central to your task. For example, I can argue with you that rugby union is a better game than football. But I can't argue you to watch a game of rugby. I need a different technique to persuade you to do something. The technique is often based on the idea that you'd be better off.

Activity 3.10

Focus on *persuading*. Remember the definition on page 77.

1 Think of things you might like to persuade some people to do. Here are some, add some more:

- stop eating so much chocolate
- take you to Disneyland
- support the Greens.

2 For each of them, write down the persuasive reason why they would be better off doing it.

Practice 3

Modelled writing: persuade, advise

Read the leaflet below, 'Food for life', which is published by the Vegetarian Society.

Work through the prompts which follow. Finding the answers to these prompts will teach you why and how the leaflet is a successful piece of persuasive writing. On this occasion, you are also given some sample responses to the prompts.

Food for Life

A Vegetarian Diet Improves Health
Research has shown that a well-balanced low-fat high-fibre vegetarian diet is healthier for you and your family.

As a vegetarian you could:

- reduce your risk from certain cancers by up to 40%
- decrease the possibility of heart disease by over 30%
- restrict your chance of suffering from kidney and gall stones, diet-related diabetes and high blood pressure
- lower your cholesterol levels and reduce health problems related to obesity
- avoid fatal diseases such as CJD, Ecoli and food poisoning.

So why not eat your way to better health?

All the nutrients you need can be easily obtained from a well-balanced vegetarian diet. In fact, research shows that a vegetarian diet is far healthier than that of a typical meat-eater. As a general rule, as long as you eat a variety of foods including grains, fruit, vegetables, beans, pulses, nuts or seeds, a small amount of fat, with or without the dairy products, your diet should be healthy and you will be getting all the nutrients you need

Food

for Life

Vegetarianism is a healthy option but it is very important to have a well-balanced diet. You could stuff your face with chips and chocolate at every meal and be vegetarian but you wouldn't be doing your health much good. It doesn't have to be rabbit food either. A varied vegetarian diet will supply all the essential nutrients you need to be fit and healthy.

continued

continued

Basic Stuff
As long as you eat a variety of foods including grains, fruit and vegetables, beans, pulses, nuts or seeds, a small amount of fat, with or without dairy products, your diet will be healthy and you will be getting all the nutrients you need.

This simple nutrition plate shows what types of food a vegetarian should eat and roughly in what quantity and proportion.

Do not worry when you stop eating meat and fish, that you might be in danger of some nutritional deficiency – this is not the case.

The plate below shows what we should eat for a balanced and healthy diet. A portion is an average serving, for example a slice of bread or two tablespoons of baked beans

5 portions daily. These provide minerals, vitamins and fibre.

Bread, cereals and potatoes
5 portions daily. This group provides us with carbohydrates, fibre, protein and some vitamins and minerals.

Milk and dairy and alternatives
2–3 portions daily. Good source of calcium, protein and some vitamins.

Eggs, beans, lentils, nuts, soya, mycoprotein (Quorn)
2–3 portions daily. This group is an important source of protein, vitamins and minerals.

Fat and sugar
0–3 portions daily. Although some fat is important in the diet, we should watch our intake.

In the know?

This is just a brief and basic example of the invaluable information we provide to members of the Vegetarian Society. We have many Information Sheets available concerning everything from pregnancy and children to hidden animal ingredients and information on the best veggie friendly places to eat and stay.
If you need to know, we'll feed you the facts.

adapted from www.vegsoc.org/health

PROMPTS

Look at the title of the leaflet.

How many meanings or interpretations can you think of for this simple phrase?

Look at the first, yellow-coloured section.

- ▶ Where and how does the writer state his topic and point of view clearly?
- ▶ How does the writer draw the reader in to what he is saying?
- ▶ What is persuasive about the contents of the yellow box?
- ▶ What comment could you make about the facts presented?
- ▶ How far do you think he has persuaded the open-minded reader by the end of the yellow section? Why?
- ▶ Who do you think this leaflet is aimed at?

Look now at the section sub-headed by the blue band.

- ▶ What 'person' is this leaflet written in?
- ▶ What does this section tell you?
- ▶ How does the writer substantiate (support) his facts?
- ▶ How does the writer put down those who are not vegetarians?

Look at the central section with the repeated title 'Food for life' which runs to the end of the plate picture.

- ▶ Explain how the writer develops the topic in this section.
- ▶ Which phrase suggests that the writer has a young audience in mind?
- ▶ Why does this vegetarian writer use the phrase 'rabbit food'?
- ▶ What is persuasive about this section?
- ▶ How has the writer dealt with the alternatives to vegetarianism in this section?

Look at the final section.

- ▶ Why is the sub-title simple but effective?
- ▶ What does the short text tell you?
- ▶ How and why is the final line effective?

Look back over the whole leaflet.

- ▶ Make some comments on the structural features of the leaflet.
- ▶ In what ways is the presentation of the leaflet interesting, effective and relevant to the audience and purpose?
- ▶ Make some comments on the varied use of language features in the text.

Possible responses

Here are some possible responses to the prompts above. Check them against what you found.

The title

- ● 'Food for Life' means food which enables you to live, as all food does, but it also suggests that the food which is to be the subject of the leaflet will lengthen your life, will not be food for illness or, worse, food which will kill you.
- ● There is the further idea that, once you have switched to vegetarian food, it will be forever – you won't go back to eating meat.

The first section

- ● The first sub-heading in the yellow box states as a fact that a vegetarian diet will improve your health and the sentence below develops this, quoting 'research'. The claim is also qualified; it must be 'well balanced, low fat, high fibre'.
- ● The writer uses the phrase 'you and your family' to involve the reader and appeal to his or her sense of responsibility.
- ● The yellow box is persuasive because it suggests that, if you don't become a vegetarian, there is a much greater

continued

continued

chance of you becoming very ill in five different ways. The word 'cancer' and 'CJD' are particularly emotive, almost frightening to people.

- The facts are not substantiated (supported), they are 'claims' rather than real facts; they may even be no more than opinions.
- The writer would have got lots of people 'on board' so far. Nobody wants to be obese or to die of cancer. This is good persuasive text and technique.
- The leaflet is aimed at everybody who is not a vegetarian. The yellow box suggests adults who are susceptible to these diseases. But young people are the real audience.

Sub-section headed by blue band

- The leaflet is written in the 'second person', the 'you' register. This appeals directly to the audience. The writer wants to persuade you to change your behaviour. The blue sub-heading asks you to eat your way to better health.
- It tells you that you can get all you need from a vegetarian diet; that you don't need meat at all.
- The writer uses the phrase 'research shows' to give some scientific support to the points being made; but it doesn't say which research, or when. Also the phrase 'general rule' sounds convincing, 'rules' after all are to be obeyed.
- He uses the phrase 'far healthier' to describe a vegetarian diet; the phrase 'typical meat-eater' is a put down, is disparaging.

Central section

- The section develops the case for eating vegetarian with information and advice. The 'variety of foods' which should be eaten, the choices and alternatives, the relative amounts are explained simply. The plate picture supports and explains the text graphically. The information is not difficult to understand. Types of food, 'quantity and proportion' are the subject

matter here; this fills in the detail which would-be vegetarians need to know.

- 'You could stuff your face with chips and chocolate' is the phrase with a young audience in mind; 'stuff your face' is a colloquialism; 'chips and chocolate' is alliterative.
- The phrase 'rabbit food' is used by non-vegetarians in a disparaging and insulting way to describe what vegetarians eat. Here a vegetarian is using it himself. In this way he reduces its effect and also states that the food he is referring to 'doesn't have to be rabbit food'.
- The section emphasises healthy eating, a varied diet including 'sweets', seems reassuring and knowledgeable and is likely to reinforce any persuading achieved earlier.
- The leaflet states that there is no danger 'when you stop eating meat and fish'. The alternatives are treated as irrelevant to healthy living. The writer is careful not to say outright that eating meat is bad for you, just that not eating it is better.

Final section

- The sub-title, 'In the know?', is really asking the reader if he is in the know or wants to be. It implies that the Vegetarian Society does have the answers if you would care to ask them.
- The text tells the reader who is responsible for the leaflet, what else they do and the range of their interests.
- The last line is short and is a pun on the word 'feed'. It also leaves the issue open. The hope is that the leaflet has been persuasive enough for you to want to find out more.

The whole leaflet

- The leaflet is highly structured and effectively so. Each section has a purpose, each sub-heading or paragraph heading is intended to involve the reader. A variety of features, such as different fonts, indents, bullet points, are used.

continued on page 96

continued from page 95

- The use of colour enhances the structural features; no section seems long or boring and each section provides new information, development or support. The pyramid picture has a particular function which is explained in the text.

- There is a mixture of pseudo (false) scientific language, factual language and everyday colloquial language. There are no difficult words or concepts. The language is suited to the target audience which is ordinary people and especially young people.

Activity 3.11

Look back at the activities on pages 84–6 to help you answer these questions.

1   Comment on how clear the leaflet is and how well it has communicated persuasive ideas and developed them.
2   a) Explain who the audience is for 'Food for life'.
    b) Is the audience kept in mind throughout? How?
3   a) Which words would you use to describe the register of the leaflet?
    b) Does the writer use more than one register? Explain.
4   a) Find examples of the use of linguistic or rhetorical devices in the leaflet.
    b) Make some changes of your own. Is the effect better or not?
5   a) Find and comment on a number of the structural devices used in 'Food for life'.
    b) How do they enhance or strengthen the leaflet?

Assessment objectives check

Although this leaflet was, of course, not written for a GCSE examination, are you satisfied that it:

- communicates clearly and imaginatively? (Assessment objective i)
- organises ideas into sentences, paragraphs and a whole text using a variety of linguistic and structural features? (Assessment objective ii)
- uses a range of sentence structures effectively with accurate punctuation and spelling? (Assessment objective iii)
- successfully persuades you of the benefits of being a vegetarian?
- advises you about the basic elements of a vegetarian diet?

Remind yourself of the definitions on page 77.

If so, then it is a successful piece in terms of persuade, advise.

Practice 4

Modelled writing: persuade, advise

Read the article below about the Shetland Islands.

Work through the prompts which follow the article. Finding the answers to these prompts will teach you why and how it is a successful piece of persuasive writing. This time you find the answers on your own, or in pair or group discussion.

 **Shetland Islands**   **more than you ever imagined**

clean and green

Shetland is one of Scotland's most environmentally conscious areas and the islands' clean and healthy environment complements the wealth of natural attractions. A new Green Tourism initiative shares the secrets of Shetland's environmental successes. Visit Shetland and enjoy these precious islands while protecting them for future generations.

A Shetland holiday will provide you with a chance to experience and enjoy the best landscapes, wildlife, traditions, and culture while avoiding damage to the environment. Whether by foot, pedal power or boat, there are many 'green' ways to enjoy your visit. Discover a diverse range of habitats, teeming with wildlife and protected on three National Nature Reserves, 72 Sites of Special Scientific Interest, and 11,600 hectares of National Scenic Area.

The islands are very fortunate to have a number of organisations with a genuine concern for the environment. These 'guardians' have an outstanding record of environmental achievement and have assembled a showcase brimming with awards.

food and drink

Enjoy a sample of Shetland's natural larder.

Shetland cuisine is based on natural, home-grown or fresh, locally-caught produce.

The islands are renowned for their rich variety of fish and shellfish and especially salmon, which enjoys an international reputation. The quality of seafood is unmis-

continued on page 98

continued from page 97

 **Shetland Islands   more than you ever imagined**

takable and the recipes are mouthwatering – escalopes of salmon with vermouth – spicy cod – grilled herring with orange – baked salmon with dill.

Another speciality is the distinctive Shetland lamb, reared on a natural diet of heather from the hills and seaweed from the shores to create a delicious flavour. The classic local dish 'Reestit Mutton' is created by salting and drying joints of lamb and is used mainly to flavour soups.

Other local produce includes a range of dairy products, delicious flavoured oat-cakes, a wide selection of fresh vegetables, fruit and herbs, fish based soups, chowders and pates and, from the most northerly brewery in Britain, a fantastic range of real ales.

cycling

Shetland has 1000 miles of road waiting to be explored. As you explore, the countryside will change from bleak heather moorland to lush green vegetation, and from stark volcanic rocks, swarming with seabirds, to valleys of fragrant wild flowers. Green fertile crofting communities, picturesque harbours with fishing boats, lochs and dramatic coastlines.

Road surfaces are excellent and the low volume of traffic on even the main roads makes cycling a pleasure. There are many miles of single track roads with regular passing places in the rural areas and most car drivers are sensitive to the presence of other road users.

All Cyclists Welcome establishments are Quality Assured by the Scottish Tourist Board and make a special effort to meet the needs of cyclists. Look out for the symbol.

Shetland forms part of the North Sea Cycle Route, 6000 km of varied and attractive courses, spanning seven countries.

adapted from www.visitshetland.com

PROMPTS

Look at the title and sub-title.

► What does the title obviously tell you?
► What does it also suggest?
► How does this affect the reader?
► What is the audience for this writing?

Read 'clean and green'.

► Who do you think has written this brochure?
► What do the writers want to emphasise about Shetland?
► How do they do this here?
► Find and explain the effects of facts and opinions in this section.
► Is there anything here which appeals to the imagination? What? How?
► Find some interesting words, some examples of an extended vocabulary.
► How many of these words and phrases do you think are persuasive?
► Is the section structured? How?
► Do the different parts of the structure connect and develop? How?

Read 'food and drink'.

► What is persuasive about this section?
► Find words and phrases which are intended to be 'mouth watering'.
► Who is the audience for this section?
► How much of this section is opinion and how much fact?
► Is there a variety of sentence forms here? Explain the effect.
► What other linguistic devices are used in this section?

Read 'cycling'

► Explain how the writers of this brochure use **imagery** in this section.
► How is this effective?
► What is persuasive about this section if you are a cyclist?
► What is persuasive if you are not a cyclist?
► What information are you given in this section?
► Is the audience for this section only cyclists? Explain.

Definition

Imagery is the use of vivid language to create pictures in the reader's mind, for example by using simile or metaphor.

Activity 3.12

Look back at the activities on pages 84–6 to help you answer these questions.

1   Comment on how clear the article is. How well has it communicated persuasive ideas and developed them?
2   a) Explain who the audience is for this article.
    b) Is the audience kept in mind throughout? How?
3   a) Which words would you use to describe the register of the article?
    b) Does the writer use more than one register? Explain.

4 a) Find examples of the use of linguistic or rhetorical devices
       in the article.
   b) Make some changes of your own. Is the effect better or not?
5 a) Find and comment on a number of the structural devices used
       in the article.
   b) How do they enhance or strengthen it?

Assessment objectives check:

Although this article was, of course, not written for a GCSE examination,
are you satisfied that it:

● communicates clearly and imaginatively? (Assessment objective i)
● organises ideas into sentences, paragraphs and a whole text using a
  variety of linguistic and structural features? (Assessment objective ii)
● uses a range of sentence structures effectively with accurate
  punctuation and spelling? (Assessment objective iii)
● successfully persuades you to visit the Shetland Islands?

Remind yourself of the definition on page 77.

If so, then it is a successful piece in terms of persuade, advise.

Practice 5

This is the question which appeared on page 78. It is connected to the reading materials about shopping and spending in Section A. The question in the exam may be similarly connected by theme to some of the reading materials for media and non-fiction.

The questions in *Practice 5*, *6* and *7* are just like the one you will meet in the examination – you are on your own.

Specimen examination question

Paper 1, Section B: Writing to argue, persuade, advise

Question 3

An article you have read in a newspaper recently states that people are spending money they don't really have and saving nothing for the future.

Write an article in reply which argues for or against the idea that people should be made by law to save for their retirement.

Practice 6

Specimen examination question

Paper 1, Section B: Writing to argue, persuade, advise

Question 3

During a recent very cold spell, Age Concern brought to the attention of the public, the fact that many elderly people suffer and die because of the sub-standard, damp and cold conditions in which they live.

Write an essay in which you argue for or against the proposal that it is the responsibility of government to improve the living conditions of these people and advise them how they should go about it.

Practice 7

Specimen examination question

Paper 1, Section B: Writing to argue, persuade, advise

Question 3

There have been a number of traffic accidents and near misses recently on a main road in a residential area near you which have involved children.

Write a letter to your council highways department which tries to persuade them that a pedestrian crossing with traffic lights is essential.

Check your answers

1   When you have completed your answers to each specimen question:
    a)   check that you have satisfied all the assessment objectives for writing (see page viii)
    b)   look at the mark scheme for writing on page xi – have you demonstrated the skills required to achieve a mark in the middle range?
2   If your teacher marks your answer, consider his or her comments and your mark. Is your mark in the middle range? Can you see why?
3   Consider what you could try to do to improve your mark, if you need to.

Paper 2

Paper 2 comprises:

- Section **A**, which examines reading
- Section **B**, which examines writing.

The paper takes 1 hour 30 minutes. Each section, as in Paper 1, is worth 15 per cent of the final mark for English.

Section A

There is one question in Section A:

- **Question 1**, which refers directly to one of the poems from other cultures and traditions provided in the pre-release booklet sent to schools before the exam. You will be asked to contrast and compare this poem with an 'unseen' poem which will appear on the examination paper.

Section B

There is one question in Section B:

- **Question 2**, in which you will be asked to produce a piece of writing to analyse, review, comment on a given topic, although you may not be asked to demonstrate all of these skills.

You will have noticed that Paper 2 has only one reading task, unlike Paper 1 which has two reading tasks. This means, of course, that you will have more time for the writing task in Paper 2. The examiner, therefore, is looking for a more developed, more carefully constructed answer to the writing question. The piece of writing expected is likely to be formal, probably in the form of an essay, and most certainly in standard English.

Section A

Section A is a test of reading. You are advised to take 45 minutes to answer the question in Section A and it is worth 15 per cent of the final mark.

The question will test your response to one of the poems from other cultures and traditions in the pre-release booklet and to one poem printed on the examination paper. Although the pre-release booklet will be the same for both Foundation and Higher Tiers, the poems on the examination papers will be different – the Higher Tier poem being rather more complex than the Foundation Tier poem.

This question, like the reading questions on Paper 1, relates to the assessment objectives for reading (see page viii). However, not all of them are relevant to this question – i, iv and v are the most important.

What this means is that you have to show, when you read and compare two poems, one of which you have never seen before, that you can:

● understand what each poem is about
● appreciate what each poet is trying to tell you, or do to you
● explain the effects of particular words, phrases and images used by each poet.

An additional requirement, always addressed in the question, is that you should be able to comment upon some of the differences between the cultures described in each of the poems.

Technical writing skills such as spelling and punctuation are not being tested in this question, and errors in these areas will not affect the final mark, but examiners will be looking for particular reading skills and will place candidates into different mark bands. These are set out on page ix.

4 Reading poetry from different cultures and traditions

This first question on Paper 2 will focus on two poems: one taken from the pre-release booklet which you will have studied in class, and one poem which you will not have seen before. In writing about them you will be asked to make comparisons about subject matter and the ways in which they are written. You will also need to be able to comment upon how they show differences between the cultures from which they are taken.

There will be no way of knowing which of the poems in the pre-release booklet will be selected by the examiner, so it will, of course, be necessary to study all of them carefully in advance.

Examiners' advice

- Remember that in the examination you will be asked to compare one of the poems in the booklet with one you have seen for the first time on the examination paper, but what matters first is that you need to know how to 'read' a poem for the purposes of this examination. *Practice 1* and *2* will help you develop this skill. *Practice 3* will then help you to develop the skills required for comparing two poems.
- As you deal with each of the poems in the pre-release booklet, it is a good idea to make notes which will help you when you come to revise for the final examination. It is strongly recommended, therefore, that you practise this note-making skill as you read and study the poems in this chapter.

In Chapter 4 you will find three example questions and three specimen examination questions:

- Practice 1, page 107 – the example question is based on the poem 'The Road to Shu is Hard' by Li Bai (China), with prompts and sample responses, to practise reading a poem
- Practice 2, page 113 – the example question is based on the poem 'The Fringe of the Sea' by A.L. Hendricks (Jamaica), with prompts, to practise reading a poem

- Practice 3, page 116 – the example question asks you to compare the two previous poems, with prompts and sample responses
- Practice 4–6, pages 123–4 – the specimen examination questions compare pairs of poems; they are based on the two previous poems plus 'The Sea Eats the Land at Home' by George Awoonor-Williams (Ghana) on page 119, 'Bwalla the Hunter' by Kath Walker (Australia, Aborigine) on page 120 and 'Palm Tree King' by John Agard (Guyana) on page 121, all without prompts.

One interesting way to tackle the questions in this chapter might be to discuss the poems in small groups and then sending 'envoys' from group to group to report on each others' findings, before coming together as a class to draw everybody's views together.

Practice 1

This is the sort of poem you may find in the pre-release booklet. The example question provides practice in how to read a poem. The prompts ask the sorts of questions you need to be able to answer in order to deal with the kind of task you will be set in the examination. These are followed by possible responses, which should give you a clear idea of the skills the examiner would be looking for.

Example question

Read the poem below, 'The Road to Shu is Hard' by the Chinese poet, Li Bai, and translated by the Indian poet and novelist, Vikram Seth.

Li Bai was born in 701 – one thousand three hundred years ago! He spent much of his life restlessly wandering and was more than once exiled from his beloved Shu (now the Chinese province of Sichuan). The kings he refers to in the poem were legendary, rather like our own King Arthur, and the earthquake he writes about was also part of ancient mythology – rather like Noah's flood, perhaps. Chengdu was the capital city of Shu.

a) What is Li Bai telling his audience?   (Assessment objective i)

b) What does he hope to achieve?   (Assessment objective i)

c) How does the poet himself feel about Shu?   (Assessment objective i)

d) How does the poet's use of language add power to his message?

(Assessment objective iv, v)

e) What effect does the cultural setting have upon your appreciation of the poem?   (Assessment objectives i, iv)

The Road to Shu is Hard

Ah! It's fearsome – oh! It's high!
The road to Shu is hard, harder than climbing to the sky.
   The kings Can Cong and Yu Fu
   Founded long ago the land of Shu.
   Then for forty-eight thousand years
   Nothing linked it to the Qin frontiers.
   White Star Peak blocked the western way.
A bird-track tried to cut across to Mount Emei –
And only when the earth shook, hills collapsed, and brave men died
Did cliff-roads and sky-ladders join it to the world outside.
Above – high peaks turn back the dragon-chariot of the sun.
Below – great whirlpools turn around the waves that rush and stun.
   Not even yellow cranes can fly across –

continued on page 108

continued from page 107

Even the clambering apes are at a loss.
At Green Mud Ridge the paths coil to and fro:
Nine twists for every hundred steps – up a sheer cliff we go.
The traveller, touching the stars, looks upwards, scared out of his wits.
He clutches his heart with a deep sigh – down on the ground he sits!
Sir, from this journey to the West, will you return some day?
How can you hope to climb the crags along this fearful way?
Mournful birds in ancient trees – you'll hear no other sound
Of life: the male bird follows his mate as they fly round and round.
You'll hear the cuckoo call in the moonlight,
Sad that the mountains are bare at night.
The road to Shu is hard, harder than climbing to the sky.
Just speak these words to someone's face – you'll see its colour fly.
A hand's breadth from the sky peaks join to crown a precipice
Where withered pines, bent upside down, lean over the abyss.
Swift rapids, wrestling cataracts descend in roaring spasms,
Pound cliffs, boil over rocks, and thunder through ten thousand chasms.

continued

continued

To face such danger and such fear,
Alas, from such a distance, Sir, what could have brought you here?
    Dagger Peak is high and steep –
    Even a single man can keep
The pass from thousands – though he may
Become a wolf or jackal – and betray.
    By day we dread the savage tiger's claws,
    By night the serpent's jaws,
    It's sharp, blood-sucking fangs bared when
    It mows down like hemp stalks the lives of men.
    Though Chengdu is a pleasure dome,
    Better to quickly turn back home.
The road to Shu is hard, harder than climbing to the sky.
Leaning, I stare into the west and utter a long sigh.

by Li Bai

Assessment objectives

The assessment objectives are given so you can see:

- why the question has been asked
- what the examiners are looking for in your answer.

Go back to page viii to remind yourself of the assessment objectives.

This section will teach you about:

- understanding the content of the poem with engagement and insight
- developing and sustaining interpretation of it
- how the writer uses linguistic effects to affect the reader
- commenting upon the cultural setting of a poem.

Examiners' advice

- The key to showing a full understanding of any piece of writing, of poetry in particular perhaps, is to be able to refer to specific words and phrases which illustrate any point you wish to make.
- It also helps to be able to use technical language.

Before answering the example question, check that you understand the following definitions and try the activities.

Definition

Rhetoric (an Ancient Greek term) is the art of persuasive speaking or writing. A **rhetorical question** is a question which does not require an answer. It is a rhetorical device, a way of trying to persuade your audience to do or believe something. It is a verbal trick — a statement is framed as a question so the listener is drawn into thinking that his opinion is being sought.

Activity 4.1

Focus on technical language: *rhetorical questions.*

1   When Li Bai asks the question: 'How can you hope to climb the crags along this fearful way?', what does he actually mean?
2   Invent a number of rhetorical questions which an angry parent might ask of an ungrateful teenager.

Definition

Compound words are made by joining two normally unrelated nouns together (usually by using hyphen) to make a striking picture, or image.

Activity 4.2

Focus on technical language: *compound words.*

1   What is the effect of describing the sun as a 'dragon-chariot'?
2   Invent a number of compound words to describe your school.

Now answer the example question:

a) What is Li Bai telling his audience?   (Assessment objective i)

b) What does he hope to achieve?   (Assessment objective i)

c) How does the poet himself feel about Shu?   (Assessment objective i)

d) How does the poet's use of language add power to his message?
                                                            (Assessment objectives iv, v)

e) What effect does the cultural setting have upon your appreciation of the poem?
                                                            (Assessment objectives i, iv)

Examiners' advice

There are no totally 'right' answers to any of the prompts. The examiner is looking for your ability to express your opinions and, for the higher grades, to justify them – to explain why you have formed these opinions. To do this, you must refer constantly to the words of the poem for evidence.

PROMPTS

▶ We seem to be listening to one half of a conversation. Who is Li Bai, or the person Li Bai pretends to be, talking to?

▶ Where, do you think, is the conversation taking place?

continued

PROMPTS continued

- What are they talking about?
- What advice is the speaker giving to the listener?
- Does Li Bai want his listener to attempt the journey?
- Why did Li Bai write this poem?
- What impression is he trying to give us of Shu and the journey to it?
- How does he feel about Shu?
- What reaction does he want from us?
- Why do you think the three exclamation marks are used in the first line?
- What do the names of the mountain features such as 'Green Mud Ridge' and 'Dagger Peak' suggest?
- What is the effect of such verbs as 'shook', 'collapsed', 'pound', 'boil' and 'thunder'?

- What do you make of adjectives like 'savage', 'sharp' and 'blood-sucking'?
- Why does the poet use rhetorical questions like: 'How can you hope to climb the crags along this fearful way?'?
- What is revealed about Li Bai's attitude to Shu by calling Chengdu a 'pleasure dome' and words such as 'leaning', 'stare' and 'sigh' in the final line?
- How does the landscape described in this poem differ from what you are used to?
- What wildlife is mentioned that is unfamiliar to you?
- How far back in time does Li Bai's knowledge of his cultural history go?

Possible responses

Here are some possible responses to the prompts. Check them against what you found.

- Li Bai appears to be speaking, or imagines that he might be speaking, to a traveller who intends to cross the mountains into Shu, probably to visit Chengdu.
- His purpose seems to be to put the traveller off, to persuade him not to go. As with all monologues, however, the poem is actually about the speaker and his attitudes.
- If you're following the AQA Specification B Literature course as well, you may already have read Browning's monologue 'My Last Duchess'. In this poem Browning pretends to be a duke criticising his late wife for her lack of loyalty and attention towards him. What Browning wants us to see, of course, is that the poem is really about the possessiveness and the lack of humanity of the duke himself. In Li Bai's poem, although he describes the landscape as dramatically and horrifically as he can, making Shu sound the most inhospitable place on earth, what he

actually reveals is his immense pride in his beloved homeland, and his longing to return, regardless of the obstacles in his path. He doesn't want the outsider to go to Chengdu, he wants to go himself – but he can't, he's in exile.

- Li Bai's picture of the road to Shu, in its attempt to put off the traveller, is hugely dramatic and owes more to fantasy than to reality. Attempt it at your peril!
- The three exclamation marks in the opening line set the tone for the whole piece – powerful, exaggerated, frightening.
- 'Green Mud Ridge' implies a hazardous, filthy mountainside where the traveller risks death by drowning or landslide. The reference to a sharp weapon in 'Dagger Peak' warns him of how he might be cut to pieces. Another named mountain is 'White Star Peak', which clearly exaggerates and makes those of us who suffer from vertigo tremble at the very thought.
- The poem is littered with powerful verbs, intended to inspire fear, such as those listed. 'Pound', 'boil' and 'thunder' actually

continued on page 112

continued from page 111

appear in one line, and together with 'roaring' in the previous line, they almost overwhelm the reader. They are certainly intended to terrify the traveller. They are also examples of onomatopoeia; the sounds of the words echo their meaning. Of course, since the poem was not originally written in English, we have to acknowledge the skill of the translator.

- Li Bai uses adjectives in a very similar way. The 'tiger's claws' inspire fear enough, but this is redoubled by describing them as 'savage'. Many of us are frightened of snakes and the picture of the 'serpent's jaws' would be enough to scare us, but to refer to them as 'sharp' and 'blood-sucking' as well turns us cold.

- There are two rhetorical questions in the poem. But they are not questions at all, here they are exclamations of disbelief. The traveller must be mad to consider such a journey!

- The final few lines are very revealing – they betray the speaker's real feelings. Virtually the only positive phrase in the entire poem, cutting right against the grain of its overall tone, is when he describes Chengdu as a 'pleasure dome'. The striking word is 'pleasure'. Does he want to be there? Does he resent the traveller's apparent freedom to go where he wants? In the final line he describes himself as 'leaning'; it's almost as though he is being pulled towards Shu by some kind of magnet. 'I stare into the west', he says, as though with an obsessed longing. The sound as well as the meaning of the final word, 'sigh', reveals the physical and emotional pain of exile.

- Your discussions in class will have made reference to lots of other words, phrases, sound effects and images which you feel are worthy of comment:
  - 'Sky-ladders' is an interesting image, as is the description of the sun as a 'dragon-chariot'.
  - 'Nine twists for every hundred steps' is a chilling and picturesque description.
  - The birds are 'mournful', an adjective we associate with death and grief.
  - The pines are 'withered', telling us even more about how inhospitable the mountains are. And so on …

- The landscape described by Li Bai is totally beyond the experience of many British people. It is described, quite deliberately, in terrifying detail, and reveals a great deal about the attitudes to life of the people who try to overcome its hardships.

- Landslides, whirlpools and death-threatening crags seem to appear at every turn – and tigers and snakes are always close at hand, as are wolves and jackals. Life in England seems so easy by comparison.

- But Li Bai would give anything to return! He longs for his homeland, steeped in its recorded traditions of forty-eight thousand years. How proud he must be of a country whose traditions extend so far back into the mists of time!

You should now have a collection of notes on this poem which will help you to answer any question put to you in the final examination.

Assessment objectives check

Check that your responses to the example question have satisfied all the relevant assessment objectives for reading poetry – i, iv, v (see page viii).

Practice 2

The next poem is, perhaps, a little less demanding than 'The Road to Shu is Hard'. It is the sort of poem you might find on the examination paper.

The example question provides practice in how to read a poem as in *Practice 1*. This time, although some prompts are provided to assist you, no responses are included. You will have to devise the answers yourself.

Example question

Read carefully the poem, 'The Fringe of the Sea'. Then answer the questions. The poet, A.L. Hendricks, was born in Kingston, Jamaica, but now lives in England.

a) What kinds of things does Hendriks love about his homeland?

(Assessment objective i)

b) What are his feelings towards Jamaica now that he lives in England?

(Assessment objective i)

c) How does his use of language add to the intensity of his feelings?

(Assessment objectives iv, v)

d) How important to our appreciation of the poem is the way of life it describes?

(Assessment objectives i, iv)

The Fringe of the Sea

We do not like to awaken
far from the fringe of the sea,
we who live upon small islands.

We like to rise up early,
quick in the agile mornings
and walk out only little distances
to look down at the water,

to know it is swaying near to us
with songs, and tides, and endless boatways,
and undulate patterns and moods.

continued on page 114

continued from page 113

We want to be able to saunter beside it
slowpaced in burning sunlight,
barearmed, barefoot, bareheaded,

and to stoop down by the shallows
sifting the random water
between assaying fingers
like farmers do with soil,

and to think of turquoise mackerel
turning with consummate grace,
sleek and decorous
and elegant in high blue chambers.

We want to be able to walk out into it,
to work in it, dive and swim and play in it,

to row and sail
and pilot over its sandless highways,
and to hear
its call and murmurs wherever we may be.

All who have lived upon small islands
want to sleep and awaken
close to the fringe of the sea.

by A. L. Hendriks

Assessment objectives

The assessment objectives are given for each part of the question so you can see:

- why the question has been asked
- what the examiners are looking for in your answer.

Go back to page viii to remind yourself of the assessment objectives.

PROMPTS

- ▶ Where do you think the poet is when he writes this piece?
- ▶ What is being described?
- ▶ How would you describe the tone, the mood of the poem?
- ▶ How does the poet feel about his homeland, Jamaica?
- ▶ What reaction does he want from his reader?
- ▶ Why does he write of 'we', not 'I'?
- ▶ Why are 'we' described as 'quick' and the mornings as 'agile'?
- ▶ What attitude to life is suggested in 'saunter' and 'slowpaced'?
- ▶ What is the reason for the constant repetition of 'bare' in 'barearmed, barefoot, bareheaded'?
- ▶ Why are the fingers described as 'assaying'? What do we normally associate this term with? What does this say about the value of the writer's homeland?
- ▶ What is the reason for the comparison with 'farmers' and 'soil'?
- ▶ 'Turquoise' is not only a colour, it is a semi-precious stone. Why do you think this adjective is used to describe the fish?

- ▶ What is suggested by 'sleek' and 'elegant'?
- ▶ What do you make of the list of verbs Hendriks applies to the sea: 'walk', 'work', 'dive', 'swim', 'play', 'row', 'sail' and 'pilot'?
- ▶ Why do you think the words of the last verse echo the words of the first?
- ▶ Does the shape of the poem suggest anything significant to you?
- ▶ Does this description of Jamaica tell us anything about the way of life the poet is recalling?
- ▶ Does it explain why he has written the piece?
- ▶ How different is the landscape described here from that described in 'The Road to Shu is Hard'?

Assessment objectives check

Check that your responses to the example question on this poem have satisfied all the relevant assessment objectives for reading (see page viii).

Practice 3

You have now looked at two poems from different times, cultures and traditions. The Chinese poem, 'The Road to Shu is Hard', is longer and possibly more complex than 'The Fringe of the Sea'. The examiner is likely to put such a poem, together with a number of others, into the pre-release booklet because he or she knows that you will have the benefit of being able to read and discuss it in the classroom with your teacher.

Let's imagine that you have just seen 'The Fringe of the Sea' for the first time on the examination paper. What kind of question might the examiner ask? It is now time to consider how to go about answering questions which require comparison. The example question in this section is just like those that you will find on the examination paper – it asks you to *compare* the two poems.

The question is followed by some advice and prompts on how to set about writing a question which requires comparison. It is assumed that you will already have dealt with the points you wish to make in your answer when you responded to the prompts in *Practice 1* and *2* .

Example question

Read the poem 'The Fringe of the Sea' and remind yourself of the poem, 'The Road to Shu' from the pre-release booklet.

Candidates are reminded to refer in their answers to the fact that the poems are from different cultures and cultures and traditions and explain how this affects their understanding and enjoyment of them.

Write a comparison of the two poems which includes:

*   an explanation of the feelings of the Jamaican man and of Li Bai

    (Assessment objectives i, iv)

*   reference to the words and tone of 'The Fringe of the Sea'

    (Assessment objectives iv, v)

*   similarities and differences between the two poems.   (Assessment objectives i, iv, v)

Assessment objectives

The assessment objectives are given for each part of the question so you can see:

● why the question has been asked
● what the examiners are looking for in your answer.

Go back to page viii to remind yourself of the assessment objectives.

Examiners' advice

● *How do you set about answering a question which requires comparison?*
You will notice immediately that the task set refers mostly to the poem on the examination paper. This is because the examiner knows that 'The Road to Shu' will have been thoroughly discussed and worked upon in the classroom. Your ability to deal with the 'unseen' poem is what the examiner is primarily concerned with, this together with your ability to compare it with something you have previously studied. In your answer, therefore, you should make sure that you spend slightly more of your time on the Jamaican poem than on the Chinese poem.

● It is always a good idea to refer to both poems in your introductory paragraph. Try the activity below.

Activity 4.3

Write an introductory paragraph in which you refer to the most striking similarity and the most striking difference between 'The Road to Shu is Hard' and 'The Fringe of the Sea'. Use the prompts below.

PROMPTS

You might like to consider:

▶ the fact that both men are separated from their homelands

▶ their feelings
▶ the differences between the settings of the two poems.

Possible response

One way of starting this particular answer, for example, might be as follows:

'Both poems, "The Fringe of the Sea" and "The Road to Shu is Hard", tell us of the feelings of people who are separated from and who long for their homelands. Although they come from very different times, cultures and traditions, both poems deal with a writer's sense of loss and regret. In severe contrast to each other, Hendriks' poem focuses on the beauty and tranquility of Jamaica whereas Li Bai describes an almost terrifying landscape'

You should now go on to deal in detail with all of the bullet points in the example question:

Write a comparison of the two poems which includes:

• an explanation of the feelings of the Jamaican man and of Li Bai
• reference to the words and tone of 'The Fringe of the Sea'
• similarities and differences between the two poems.

Make use of the points raised in *Practice 1* and *2*. These should give you more than you need to fulfil this task. Write your answer in continuous prose.

Check your answer

1 When you have completed your answer to the example question:
   a) check that you have satisfied all the relevant assessment objectives for reading poetry – i, iv, v (see page viii)
   b) look at the mark scheme for reading poetry on page ix – which mark band do you think your answer is in? Explain why.
2 If your teacher marks your answer, consider his or her comments and how your mark fits in the mark scheme. Which mark band is your answer in? Can you see why?
3 Consider what you could try to do to move into a higher mark band.

The Sea Eats the Land at Home

At home the sea is in the town,
Running in and out of the cooking places,
Collecting the firewood from the hearths
And sending it back at night;
The sea eats the land at home.
It came one day at the dead of night,
Destroying the cement walls,
And carried away the fowls,
The cooking-pots and the ladles,
The sea eats the land at home;
It is a sad thing to hear the wails,
And the mourning shouts of the women,
Calling on all the gods they worship,
To protect them from the angry sea.
Aku stood outside where her cooking-pot stood,
With her two children shivering from the cold,
Her hands on her breast,
Weeping mournfully.
Her ancestors have neglected her,
Her gods have deserted her,
It was a cold Sunday morning,
The storm was raging,
Goats and fowls were struggling in the water,
The angry water of the cruel sea;
The lap-lapping of the dark water at the shore,
And above the sobs and the deep and low moans
Was the eternal hum of the living sea.
It has taken away their belongings,
Adena has lost the trinkets which
Were her dowry and her joy
In the sea that eats the land at home,
Eats the whole land at home.

by George Awoonor-Williams

Bwalla the Hunter

In the hard famine time, in the long drought
Bwalla the hunter on walkabout,
Lubra and children following slow,
All proper hungry long time now.

No more kangaroo out on the plain,
Gone to other country where there was rain.
Couldn't find emu, couldn't find seed,
And the children all time cry for feed.

They saw great eagle come through the sky
To his big stick gunya in a gim near by,
Fine young wallaby carried in his feet:
He bring tucker for his kids to eat.

Big fella eagle circled slow,
Little fella eagles fed below.
'Gwa!' said Bwalla the hunter, 'he
Best fella hunter, better than me.'

He dropped his boomerang. 'Now I climb,
All share tucker in the hungry time.
We got younks too, we got need –
You make fire and we all have feed.'

Then up went Bwalla lika a native cat,
All the blackfellows climb like that.
And when he look over big nest rim
Those young ones all sing out at him.

They flapped and spat, they snapped and clawed,
They plenty wild with him, my word,
They shrilled at tucker-thief big and brown,
But Bwalla took wallaby and then climbed down.

by Kath Walker

Palm Tree King

Because I come from the West Indies
certain people in England seem to think
I is a expert on palm trees.

So not wanting to sever dis link
with me native roots (know what ah mean?)
or to disappoint dese culture vulture
I does smile cool as seabreeze

and say to dem
which specimen
you interested in
cause you talking
to the right man
I is palm tree king
I know palm tree history
like de palm o me hand
In fact me navel strin
bury under a palm tree

If you think da queen could wave
you ain't seen nothing yet
till you see the Roystonea Regia
– that is the royal palm –
with she crown of leaves
waving calm-calm
over the blue Caribbean carpet
nearly 100 feet of royal highness

But let we get down to business
Tell me what you want to know
How tall a palm tree does grow?
What is the biggest coconut I ever see?
What is the average length of the leaf?
Don't expect me to be brief
cause palm tree history
is a long-long story
Anyway why you so interested
in length and circumference?
That kind of talk so ordinary
That don't touch the essence
of palm tree mystery
That is no challenge
to a palm tree historian like me

continued on page 122

continued from page 121

If you insist on statistics
why you don't pose a question
with some mathematical profundity?

Ask me something more tricky
like if a American tourist with a camera
take 9 minutes to climb a coconut tree
how long it take a English tourist without a camera
would take to climb the same coconut tree?

That is problem pardner
Now ah coming harder

If 6 straw hat
and half a dozen bikini
multiply by the same number of coconut tree
equal one postcard
how many square miles of straw hat
you need to make a tourist industry?

That is problem pardner
Find the solution
and you got a revolution

But before you say anything
let I palm tree king
give you dis warning
Ah want de answer in metric
it kind of rhyme with tropic
Beside it sound more exotic.

by John Agard

Practice 4

You could discuss this question, and those in *Practice 5* and *6*, in class or you could write answers as though you were in the exam. If you do write, try to answer in 45 minutes.

From now on, there are no prompts – you are on your own.

Specimen examination question

Paper 2, Section A: Poetry from different cultures

Question 1

Read the poems 'The Fringe of the Sea' (page 113) and 'The Sea Eats the Land at Home' (page 119).

Candidates are reminded to refer in their answers to the fact that the poems are from different cultures and how this has affected their understanding and enjoyment of them.

Write a comparison of the two poems which includes:

*   an explanation of the disaster on the Ghanean coast
*   the language and tone of Williams' poem
*   the contrast between the two poets' attitudes towards the sea in their native lands.

Practice 5

Specimen examination question

Paper 2, Section A: Poetry from different cultures

Question 1

Read the poems 'Bwalla the Hunter' (page 120) and 'Palm Tree King' (page 121).

Candidates are reminded to refer in their answers to the fact that the poems are from different cultures and how this has affected their understanding and enjoyment of them.

Write a comparison of the two poems which includes:

*   an explanation of how Bwalla deals with a problem
*   how Agard fights back against the problem of racist abuse
*   the different versions of the English language presented in the poems.

Practice 6

Specimen examination question

Paper 2, Section A: Poetry from different cultures

Question 1

Read 'The Palm Tree King' (page 121) and 'The Sea Eats the Land' (page 119).

Candidates are reminded to refer in their answers to the fact that the poems are from different cultures and how this has affected their understanding and enjoyment of them.

Write a comparison of the two poems which includes:

- the way in which Agard uses humour to attack racists
- the way in which Williams uses language to describe the desperate plight of his country.

Check your answers

1 When you have completed your answers to each specimen question:
   a) check that you have satisfied all the relevant assessment objectives for reading poetry – i, iv, v (see page viii)
   b) look at the mark scheme for reading poetry on page ix – which mark band do you think your answer is in? Explain why.
2 If your teacher marks your answer, consider his or her comments and how your mark fits in the mark scheme. Which mark band is your answer in? Can you see why?
3 Consider what you could try to do to move into a higher mark band.

Section B

Question 2 in Section B is a test of writing. Like the writing question on Paper 1, it is worth 15 per cent of the total marks for the examination. It is very important to note, however, that the examiner expects you to spend 45 minutes on this section of Paper 2, a little longer than is available to you to answer the writing question on Paper 1.

The assessment objectives for this question are the same as for the writing question on Paper 1 (see page viii). The mark scheme for grade C is set out on pages xi–xii.

5 Writing to analyse, review, comment

In the exam question the examiner might set a task which mentions all three of these words or, on occasions, just two. What, then, do they mean? What do you have to do?

Definitions

- **Review** By asking you to review an event or situation, the examiner is asking you to take a very close look at it — literally, to look at it again, with a close critical eye.

- **Analyse** When you are asked to analyse you are being asked to show that you can make comparisons, that you can point out the advantages and disadvantages of a particular course of action or of a particular state of affairs.

- **Comment** means to give your own point of view.

The topic of a *review* question will always be one of which most teenagers have personal experience or about which they are likely to have an opinion. The tasks set tend to deal with your own lives, asking you to look at issues such as teenage lifestyles, your local environment, your experience of school, your hopes for the future, your personal view of right and wrong. In every case the task will require you to deal with a situation about which opinions will vary.

When you are asked to *analyse*, you are *not* being asked to argue or persuade (these skills are tested elsewhere); you are being asked to show an awareness of what the issues and alternatives are. *Balance* is what is required: showing your readers that there are two or more ways of looking at an issue. Although you are bound to be subjective (expressing your personal point of view) at times, you should also attempt to be objective (seeing the situation through others' eyes) if you can. Demonstrating this key skill is the essence of the task. To make sure you have fully understood these terms, try Activity 5.1.

Activity 5.1

Focus on *fact* and *opinion*. Remember the definitions on page 10.

1 Make one objective comment about the town in which you live – a fact.
2 Make one subjective comment – an opinion.

Comment is unavoidable! When you review and analyse a situation or issue, it is almost impossible to stop yourself from commenting – that is, giving your own point of view. The task will not require you to come to a particular conclusion – analysis is more about balance – but you may want to make your own view clear to the reader.

The best way to demonstrate these points is by taking a careful look at some 'real' pieces of writing in *Practice 1* and *2*, which actually set out to analyse, review and comment.

Examiners' advice

- A fuller answer, showing especially careful consideration of the topic, will be expected for this question.
- On some occasions the examiner may ask you to write for particular readers – of a school magazine, or of a local newspaper, for example – but this will not always be the case. It is quite likely that you will be expected to write a formal essay on the topic set.
- Before writing you will have to make two very important decisions:
    - Tone: Should I take a serious or a light-hearted approach to the subject?
    - Language register: Should I write in formal, Standard English, or does the topic lend itself to a less formal, colloquial style?

To help you understand these ideas, try the following activities.

Activity 5.2

Focus on *tone*. Remember the definition on page 19.

1 Explain to a friend in a light-hearted tone that whether you do well or do badly in your GCSE examinations simply does not matter.
2 Imagine you are a parent using a serious tone to convince a teenager that exams actually are important.

Activity 5.3

Focus on *language register*. Remember the definition on page 84.

Imagine that David Beckham scores a goal in the last minute to win the World Cup. Neither your English teacher nor your best friend was able to watch the match.

Describe the goal to each person in turn, using what you consider to be an appropriate register.

In this chapter two pieces of modelled writing, one example question and three specimen examination questions are provided:

● Practice 1, page 130 – the modelled writing is 'A wounded world', a leader article, with prompts and sample responses
● Practice 2, page 135 – the modelled writing is 'This epic wizardry dwarfs all the rest', a film review, with prompts
● Practice 3, page 138 – an example question, with advice and examples
● Practice 4–6, page 144 – specimen examination questions, exactly like the examination – you are given no help at all.

Before you continue, remind yourself of the assessment objectives for writing on page viii.

Practice 1

Modelled writing: review, analyse, comment

Read the following article, written by one of the editorial team of *The Guardian* on New Year's Eve, 2001. Then work through the prompts that follow. (You could do this as a class discussion.) Finding the answers to these prompts will teach you why and how this is an effective piece of writing which seeks to analyse, review, comment. On this occasion, you are given some possible responses.

There is no way of knowing whether the article was written by a man or a woman. Unfortunately there is no alternative pronoun in the English language to 'he' or 'she' so, with apologies, 'he' is used throughout the commentary.

A Wounded World
America's pain was felt across the globe

IF AL GORE had been elected president of the United States, one of his pledges was to authorize the launch of an orbiting satellite webcam in space. Its simple purpose would be to beam back live pictures of the Earth to the Earth, for all humankind to marvel at. The project was mocked by US Republicans, who seem to see space in military not existential terms, and it was quickly redlined by George Bush, who does what he is told. Yet if the GoreCam had somehow been in the skies, what would it have shown us about our world in 2001?

continued

continued

By day, it would reveal a planet as awesomely beautiful and abundant in natural wealth as ever. Perhaps it would be a little greener here, a little more arid there, the ice cap less in evidence than before around the poles. Yet still, in spite of all this, the sight would be a continuing source of wonder and inspiration. By night, more difficult questions would arise. The camera would show the Americans and Europe ablaze and resplendent with lights, burning electricity like there was no tomorrow. Meanwhile, all of Africa and large parts of Asia would lie dark and unlit as if during a wartime bombing raid, a fate that one or two places down there would actually be enduring. From time to time also, the circling camera might pick out distant evidence of interruptions to the essential continuation of the planet: an arc of bush fires around Sydney, a plume of ash climbing from the crater of an erupting Etna, an uncoiled hurricane hurtling across Cuba and, one crystalline morning in early autumn, a thin wisp of smoke rising from the southern end of Manhattan towards the heavens.

Down here on the ground, we have lived the last part of the old year in the dark shadow of the smoke from Manhattan. It was mesmerizing to look at and it brought into the daylight some of the troubling questions that the orbiting space camera would have exposed only at night. Yet we should not doubt what we saw. The event that we watched and grappled to comprehend was the most deliberate act of human wickedness in the west for a generation. Of greater immediate significance, it was also the gravest act of aggression against the United States in the more than two centuries of its history. As such, it was not just a challenge to the supremacy of a nation whose wealth, values and culture have come to dominate the planet more totally than Empires from Alexander the Great to Stalin ever did. To

Americans – and not just to Americans, but also to those millions around the world who live, or aspire to live, the life of liberty, opportunity, prosperity and happiness that America, however imperfectly represents – the attacks struck at much of what is wonderful and worthwhile about life. They could not possibly go unpunished. Nor could they conceivably be permitted to recur. If those just aims have been even partially achieved in the weeks since the attacks, then the wounded world is now in a small way a better place.

A better place? Let us begin the new year by hoping so. And yet the continuities, both for good and for evil, are imposing. Just as the planet's natural abundance is still there every morning, so also is the inequality of the life that the human race lives upon it. The world is infinitely more complex and extraordinary than the world as seen from a distant, silent satellite or from a hurt and self-absorbed America. In this country we will all spend many fulfilling hours this coming year absorbed in everything from the euro and the reform of public services to the World Cup and the latest piece of vulgar exhibitionism by meretricious celebs. But let us at least try to get these things in perspective. The war fought by the United States in Afghanistan was a war involving nations whose per capita GDP is $33,900 and $800 respectively, whose infant mortality rates are seven per thousand and 154 per thousand, whose average daily calorie intakes are 3,642 (the second highest in the world) and 1,523 (the second lowest), where average life expectancy is 76 and 44, and where 100% of the population has access to safe water, compared with only 12%. If we have learned a little more this year than we thought possible about the human capacity for evil, let us also remember at the start of the new one that there is much to examine and act on in our own better values too.

The Guardian, 31 December 2001

This piece, written on the last day of the year, seeks to discuss whether or not the world is a better place at the end of 2001 than it was at the end of the previous year. The writer looks at the world as a whole, seeking to *review* the major events, to *analyse* what he regards as the most important of them, and to *comment* on the situation as he finds it.

Let us look at how he goes about this.

PROMPTS

- ▶ How does the writer makes it clear in his introductory paragraph what he is going to review?
- ▶ How is the article structured? How are topic sentences used at the beginning of each paragraph?
- ▶ What are the events he considers significant in the year 2001, and the one he analyses particularly carefully?
- ▶ What is the global issue he analyses closely and considers to be the most urgent?

- ▶ What are the writer's comments on the events and issues he deals with, and the point of view which these reveal?
- ▶ What is the overall tone of the article?
- ▶ How would you describe the language register used by the writer?
- ▶ What do you find interesting about the ways in which the writer uses language to engage the interest and, at times, the emotions of his readers?

Possible responses
Here are some possible responses to the prompts above. Check them against what you found.

- ● The introductory paragraph makes it clear that the writer is going to concern himself with global issues. He does this by asking us to imagine that we are in the position of a webcam camera looking down on what has been going on in the world. We are, as it were, the all-seeing lens.

- ● The structure of the passage after this introduction is very clear: the second paragraph presents us with a very positive picture of the world in general, although hinting at something darker, and then lists the (mostly) natural disasters which have occurred; the third paragraph inevitably deals more fully with the most important event of the year; the fourth paragraph deals with the most important issue.

- ● Each paragraph begins with a topic sentence – the writer makes it absolutely clear what he is going to be dealing with in the following sentences. His aim is total clarity, to make the reader's job as straightforward as possible.

- ● Within paragraphs, in order to show balance, the writer uses co-ordinating connectors which take us from one point of view to the other. Examples are: 'Yet' (paragraph 1); 'Meanwhile' (paragraph 2); 'And yet' (paragraph 3); 'But let us at least try' (paragraph 4).

- ● The important global events mentioned are, apart from a reference to the aftermath of the American presidential election, mostly natural disasters, the likes of which are likely to occur in any given year. The world was forced to endure in 2001 bushfires in Australia, a major volcanic eruption and one particularly powerful hurricane.

continued

continued

- The most important event of the year, however, the writer makes it clear, was not a natural disaster, but a man-made one. He devotes a whole complex paragraph to the events in New York on 11 September, and to his reflections upon what has happened as a result.
- The global issue he focuses upon, introducing it in the second paragraph and developing it in the fourth, is what he sees as the inequality of opportunity for different peoples in the world; the vast wealth enjoyed by some nations and the poverty endured by others.
- The writer's comments are an important feature of the article. It is, of course, important to note that they represent his own and his employer's views but that they are by no means universal: you may very well disagree with him. They are opinions, not facts. He has opinions on all he discusses and analyses and lets us know, when he has weighed it up, what he agrees and disagrees with. He appears to be at pains, however, to achieve balance. Some of his views are that:
  - Mr Bush and the Republican Party have different values from his own
  - the planet Earth remains, although no longer perfect, a beautiful planet
  - America and Europe are very wasteful
  - the attack on America was totally unjustified
  - the American response, though regrettable, was justified on the grounds that nothing like this attack should ever be allowed to happen again
  - the wealth enjoyed by America and Europe enables them to lead untroubled but trivial lives
  - many peoples in the world, including the Afghans, have no time for trivia and are left to lead their lives in abject poverty.

- The tone of the passage is almost entirely serious and increasingly grave. The author allows us the tiniest glimpse of humour in the opening paragraph when he suggests that Mr Bush merely follows the orders of others. He begins the second paragraph by presenting us with a positive, briefly colourful view of the planet, but he then goes on to discuss what he considers to be the important issues in a very solemn tone.
- The language register used by the writer is very formal, entirely in keeping with the tone. He uses standard English throughout. Every sentence is most carefully constructed. There are no abbreviations whatever, and scarcely an instance of colloquial language or slang. The vocabulary, though generally not difficult, is very precise. He is at pains to see that there is no possibility of his being misunderstood. He does not seek to inflame the reader's emotions by means of highly dramatic language or rhetorical questions, graphic descriptions or vicious personal attacks on individuals or groups. He expresses a personal (subjective) view but does not set out to force it upon the reader; the reader is asked to reflect upon the article, to match his or her own views against those expressed, and to come to a personal conclusion. In his attempt to be objective and to be seen to present a balanced view he very carefully avoids the use of the personal pronoun, 'I'.
- The writer's use of language is varied. You may have pointed out, amongst others, some of these:
  - the positive and encouraging picture of the planet in 'awesomely beautiful and abundant in nature' and 'wonder and inspiration' in the second paragraph
  - how 'ablaze and resplendent' contrasts with 'dark and unlit' when comparing the ways of life in different parts of the world

continued on page 134

continued from page 133

— the blunt frankness in the choice of words such as 'wickedness' and 'evil'
— the uplifting effect of the list of values he holds dear and which many of us are lucky enough to take for granted: 'the life of liberty, opportunity, prosperity and happiness'

— the scornful tone adopted when suggesting that in the so-called developed world we concern ourselves only with trivia — at the end of his list he writes: 'the latest piece of vulgar exhibitionism by meretricious celebs'
— the use of numbers and statistics to contrast two different ways of life in the final paragraph — once again using a list to add emphasis.

Assessment objectives check

Although, this article was, of course, not written for a GCSE examination, are you satisfied that it:

● communicates clearly and imaginatively? (Assessment objective i)
● organises ideas into sentences, paragraphs and a whole text using a variety of linguistic and structural features? (Assessment objective ii)
● uses a range of sentence structures effectively with accurate punctuation and spelling? (Assessment objective iii)
● successfully reviews major events of 2001?
● analyses these events and comments upon them?

Remind yourself of the definitions on page 127.

If so, then it is a successful piece in terms of analyse, review, comment.

Practice 2

Modelled writing: analyse, review, comment

Read the following extract from a film review, published in *The Mail on Sunday* within days of the film's release.

When you have read the piece, discuss the following questions:

- What is the writer, Matthew Bond, seeking to do in this review?
- How is the article structured? What aspects of the film does he analyse, and what comments does he make?
- How and why do his tone and language register differ from 'A Wounded World'?

Remember that on this occasion, although you will be given prompts, it is up to you to find the 'answers' for yourself. They will help you to understand just what skills are required to produce a piece of writing which seeks to analyse, review, comment.

This epic wizardry dwarfs all the rest

There is a time and a place for **The Lord of the Rings** and, by and large, that time is the messy bedroom of an introspective teenager. That's certainly how it was for me. I read it, I was consumed by it, I even went through a short period of adolescent mourning when I finished it and discovered that J.R.R. Tolkien was dead and that there wouldn't be a sequel. But I got over it – most of us do.

Some, indeed, will be so over their Tolkien experience that they won't see the merit in Peter Jackson's ambitious film adaptation.

Matthew Bond

Film of the week

Actors rushing around pretending to be Hobbits, wizards and elves ... all that cod-mythological guff about an all-powerful ring ... three hours long but still nowhere near the end of the book. You're joking aren't you?

Well no, Jackson isn't joking. Faithful to the story and the descriptions, but not necessarily the fine detail of the book, he has conjured up a film that is visually quite stunning; certainly sustains the odd metaphor or two; and, now and again, even manages to be gently moving. It should delight all but the most tryingly pedantic of Tolkien fans.

On the other hand, there is no getting away from the fact that it is three hours long and that somewhere in the Mines of Moria it seems to turn into a very long version of Jason and the Argonauts. Only with better special effects.

Ah, the special effects. Cleverly – or possibly inadvertently – Jackson doesn't hit us with his best computer-generated shot right at the start. As a sonorous voice-over fills us with a bit of basic ring mythology, the goodies and some ugly-looking bad-

continued on page 136

continued from page 135

Above: *Ian McKellen as Gandalf*

dies line up for battle, just as they do in The Mummy Returns. Seen it, I thought – not impressed.

But by the time Gandalf (Ian McKellen) and Saruman (Christopher Lee) have had their physics-defying fight, the orcs have started their massive tunneling and Cate Blanchett has floated around the arboreal paradise of Lothlorien in her best elfin nightie, I was completely bowled over.

Without a doubt, and despite their eventual overuse, they are the best special effects we have seen this year. They make Harry Potter's Quidditch game look … well, rather dull. …

Jackson doesn't really secure a knock-out performance from any of his cast but they are all more than competent and, you could argue, act more as an ensemble than as individuals. And yet, when the pace does start to drag a little as we leave the stunning landscapes of the New Zealand locations to enter the Mines of Moria and the energy-sapping third hour, what we need is individuals, characters you really care about, and I'm not sure we really have them.

Paradoxically, given the film's inordinate length, Jackson may actually not have given himself enough time to establish some of the later characters. The actual Fellowship of the Ring – four Hobbits, two humans (Aragorn and Boromir, played by Sean Bean), Gandalf, Gimli the dwarf and Legolas the elf – doesn't come into being until well over an hour-and-a-half has passed. And once they do team up to take the ring back to Mordor they inevitably spend more time running away from ancient fiery demons than they do chatting.

But there is no denying Jackson's towering achievement in bringing a film of such immense scale and fine detail to the screen. Certainly, it stands a decent chance of winning Best Picture at the Academy Awards (nothing Hollywood likes more than a really big picture) and securing a Best Adapted Screenplay nomination for Jackson and his co-writers, as well as picking up a handful of technical nominations for production design, special effects, sound and costume.

Sentimental old things that Academy members are, there may even be a Best Supporting Actor nomination for McKellen. We shall see.

Me, I'm just content to have been so spectacularly reunited with an old, almost forgotten friend. Tolkien's story no longer moves me as it once did, but as a magical movie reminder this takes an awful lot of beating.

adapted from *The Mail on Sunday*, 16 December 2001

Look at the questions once again and discuss them, using the prompts to guide you:

● What is the writer, Matthew Bond, seeking to do in this review?
● How is the article structured? What aspects of the film does he analyse, and what comments does he make?
● How and why do his tone and language register differ from 'A Wounded World'?

PROMPTS

What's Matthew Bond, the reviewer, trying to do here?

► Is the piece one-sided, or does he attempt balance?
► What other films does he refer to? Why?
► Would this piece help you decide whether or not to go and see the film?

The structure of the article: what are the aspects of the film he analyses and the comments he makes?

► Does he think the film is an accurate representation of the book?
► What does he think of the special effects?
► What does he think of the acting?
► Does he find the characters convincing?
► What does he think will be the response of the film industry?

► Does he like the film?
► What co-ordinating connectors (e.g. 'On the other hand ...') does he use to move from one point of view to another?

How do the tone and the language register of this article differ from 'A Wounded World'?

► What examples can you find of humour in this review? How do these show a difference in tone from 'A Wounded World'?
► What examples of everyday conversational (colloquial) language can you find?
► Can you find examples of Bond allowing himself to be obviously subjective rather than objective?
► Do you think the tone and use of language are appropriate for such a piece of writing?
► Why, or why not? Give examples.

Assessment objectives check

Although, this article was, of course, not written for a GCSE examination, are you satisfied that it:

● communicates clearly and imaginatively? (Assessment objective i)
● organises ideas into sentences, paragraphs and a whole text using a variety of linguistic and structural features? (Assessment objective ii)
● uses a range of sentence structures effectively with accurate punctuation and spelling? (Assessment objective iii)
● successfully reviews the film 'The Lord of the Rings'?
● analyses it and comments upon it?

Remind yourself of the definitions on page 127.

If so, then it is a successful piece in terms of analyse, review, comment.

Activity 5.4

Now that you have read two very different kinds of article which seek to review, analyse, comment, what features can you identify that seem to be typical of such writing? List them.

Practice 3

In Activity 5.4 you may well have identified the following as some of the features of writing which seeks to analyse, review, comment:

- Writers present us with pieces of information about their chosen subject.
- They aim to present a balanced point of view of their topic.
- Personal points of view are unavoidable, but do not dominate.
- Writers structure their writing clearly and logically, usually in paragraphs, usually dealing with one point at a time.
- Co-ordinating connectors (such as 'On the one hand … on the other hand') are used to help move from one point of view to another.
- Before writing careful decisions have to be made about tone and language register, to ensure that they are appropriate for the subject and audience.
- Attention must be paid to spelling and punctuation. In the examination room this should be done as your final read-through before handing in your completed paper.

Let us now look at an example of a question that you might find on an examination paper and consider in detail how to go about answering it.

Example question

After GCSE examinations important decisions have to be made by those who wish to continue their education. Should they, for example, stay on at school in the Sixth Form, or should they leave and go to the local college of further education?

Write an essay, based on your own views and on what you might have heard from others, in which you analyse and comment upon the advantages and disadvantages of each course of action. (Assessment objectives i, ii, iii)

Examiners' advice

In preparing to answer the question, try to make use of the features identified above. We will take each one in turn below. Some examples have been given to help you further.

Ways of gathering and presenting information

It helps, of course, to be well informed about your subject. The examiner will do his or her best to ensure that virtually all young people will be informed to some extent but cannot possibly guarantee that everyone will be an expert. Consequently some candidates will be able to draw upon more 'evidence' than others. It is important to note, however, that this is an *English* examination – the examiner is looking for how well you deal with what you have to say rather than with the points themselves. You will not be penalised if your knowledge of the topic is not as fully developed as that of other candidates.

Most of us are impressed by statistics, and we seldom check them. They are used as a rhetorical device to help convince. If you were to *make up* statistics, who would know?

Activity 5.5

1 Invent statistics which suggest that most sixteen-year-olds leave school to go to college.
2 Invent statistics which suggest exactly the opposite.

Activity 5.6

1 Invent a quotation from an imaginary college principal, arguing that college is a more effective choice than staying on at school.
2 Invent a quotation from an imaginary headteacher arguing the opposite case.

However well-informed you are about the topic, you should begin by gathering together the points you wish to make. This need take only five minutes or so, but it is essential to organise your ideas before you even think of starting to write your essay.

Probably the best way to do this is to use a brainstorming technique. Some people like to make lists and others prefer to make spider diagrams.

Brainstorming: lists
When you are brainstorming, of course, ideas do not necessarily come in logical order, nor do they come neatly arranged in categories such as 'good' and 'bad' – they occur to you almost at random. They need to be arranged into the order in which you intend to deal with them afterwards, simply by adding a number. In this way you can see the structure of your piece, paragraph by paragraph.

For example, if Matthew Bond had used this technique to prepare the first draft of his film review (*Practice 2*), it might have looked something like this:

Lord of the Rings – film review		*Good*	*Bad*
Special effects	4	orcs tunnelling	opening
The book	1	loved it!	nearly forgotten it
		Exciting	silly plot
Characters	7	Gandalf	The Fellowship
		Saruman	
Setting	6	New Zealand	
Fair to book?	2	Story	detail
Length	3		verrrrrry long!
Actors	5	Ian McKellen	Sean Bean?

Similar films: Jason and the Argonauts, Harry Potter, The Mummy Returns

Brainstorming: spider diagrams
If Matthew Bond had used a spider diagram, it might have looked like this:

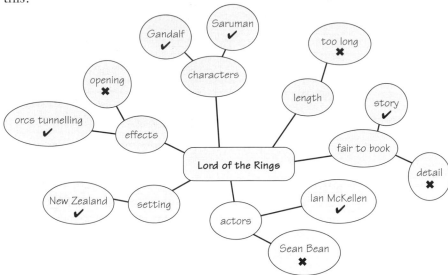

Let us, then, look at how you might go about gathering together the points to be made in answer to the example question:

After GCSE examinations important decisions have to be made by those who wish to continue their education. Should they, for example, stay on at school in the Sixth Form, or should they leave and go to the local college of further education?

Write an essay, based on your own views and on what you might have heard from others, in which you analyse and comment upon the advantages and disadvantages of each course of action.

Activity 5.7

Produce a list or a spider diagram of the points you would wish to make on this topic

Here are one or two ideas to get you started, but working in pairs or on your own you will find yourself able to generate far more points:

	School	College
Friends	Old and close	New faces
Courses	Traditional	More varied
Facilities		
Teachers		
Hours		

Try to produce a spider diagram if you prefer this approach.

Balance

The list or spider diagram you have produced certainly assists here; it almost forces you to look at both sides of the issue. Take the issue of friends, for example. One of the advantages of staying on at school is that you will still be surrounded by most of the close friends you have made over a number of years. On the other hand, if you go to college you are likely to make a whole new set of friends – then you'll have two lots of friends. So, which is better? Remember – you're not necessarily being asked to draw conclusions, simply to identify the issues. You don't have to answer the question. What about facilities?

Activity 5.8

Make sure that your list or spider diagram contains both favourable and unfavourable comments about the facilities in your school compared with the local college of further education.

Personal point of view

This is probably unavoidable. At the end of your essay the likelihood is that you will recommend one course of action in preference to the other. Remember, though, that this is not as important as showing that you understand all the options.

Logical structure

The information-gathering process – the list or spider diagram – is very useful here. Numbering your points in the order they should be dealt with will produce an ordered structure.

The opening paragraph is very important, of course; in it you must clearly state your intentions, explaining exactly what it is you are going to analyse, review and comment upon. Both of the modelled examples in *Practice 1* and *2* do precisely this.

Activity 5.9

Write the opening paragraph of your essay, in which you make it absolutely clear what the issue is that you intend to deal with.

For example, you could begin with:

'One of the most important decisions to be taken after GCSE examinations is exactly what to do next. Leave school and get a job, or continue in education? If you *do* want to carry on studying, where should it be? School or college? Opinions vary: there are those who …'

Co-ordinating connectors

These are ways of moving from one point of view to another. In the last sentence above you will see one of these – 'there are those who …'. Later in the paragraph you might use: 'There are those, however, who believe that ...', and this would introduce a different point of view.

In writing which seeks to analyse, review, comment such devices are remarkably common.

Activity 5.10

1 Complete the following sentences to use in response to the example question:
   a) On the one hand ...
   b) On the other hand ...
   c) Most people believe ...
   d) My personal opinion, however, ...
2 Write some more relevant sentences using co-ordinating connectors of your own.

Tone and language register

Should you adopt a formal or a more chatty, colloquial style?

The way in which the question is phrased usually points you in the right direction. On this particular occasion you have been asked to 'Write an essay ...'.

Essays are normally written in formal, standard English, rather like the newspaper articles in *Practice 1* and *2* – the leader article and the film review. You will notice that 'A Wounded World' is particularly formal in approach – largely because of the seriousness of the topic.

A formal, serious style is probably the safest to adopt.

Activity 5.11

Select one of the points from your list or spider diagram and write a paragraph in a formal style, using standard English.

For example, you might write:

> 'Colleges of higher education are specifically intended for older students of all abilities and interests and they are therefore able to offer a great variety of courses, some traditional and others vocational. Most schools, on the other hand ...'

However, you may, if you wish, adopt a much more informal language register, particularly if you decide to adopt a more light-hearted tone. This is more difficult to sustain throughout an entire piece, particularly if you are looking for balance too, but a start like this is bound to attract the examiner's interest.

Activity 5.12

Taking the same point as you selected for the previous activity, write a paragraph in a more informal, perhaps more light-hearted register.

This might have been the outcome:

'Stay at school! Are you joking? Have you met Mr Jones, my French teacher ...'

Sometimes, of course, the examiner will make the decision easier for you by suggesting that you write an article for a school magazine or write a presentation for the governors of the school. You will be given a specific, named audience and decisions about register and tone will almost be made for you.

Spelling and punctuation

Dictionaries are not allowed in English examinations, so it is impossible to check exactly. You should, however, read through your essay one last time doing your best to eliminate spelling and punctuation errors, and making sure that every one of your sentences makes sense.

Now write your answer to the example question:

After GCSE examinations important decisions have to be made by those who wish to continue their education. Should they, for example, stay on at school in the Sixth Form, or should they leave and go to the local college of further education?

Write an essay, based on your own views and on what you might have heard from others, in which you analyse and comment upon the advantages and disadvantages of each course of action.

Check your answer
1   When you have completed your answer to the example question:
    a) check that you have satisfied all the assessment ojectives for writing (see page viii)
    b) look at the mark scheme for writing on page xi – have you demonstrated the skills required to achieve a mark in the middle range?
2   If your teacher marks your answer, consider his or her comments and your mark. Is your mark in the middle range? Can you see why?
3   Consider what you could try to do to improve your mark, if you need to.

Practice 4

In *Practice* sections 4, 5 and 6, you are given questions just as you would find them in the exam. No help is given – you are on your own.

Specimen examination question

Paper 2, Section B: Writing to analyse, review, comment

Question 2
The government has allowed your school a grant for one of two purposes: either to build a new sports hall or an arts centre for drama, music, dance, etc. – neither of which your school has at the moment.

The headteacher and governors, in order to help them with their decision, have asked a number of students, including yourself, to analyse the options and to write to them with your comments. Write a letter in response to the Chair of Governors.

Practice 5

Specimen examination question

Paper 2, Section B: Writing to analyse, review, comment

Question 2
Some people like to take their holidays abroad and some people prefer to stay in their own country. Your local newspaper is offering a prize for the most interesting article on the subject.

Reviewing your own experiences, and referring to the opinions of others, write your entry for the competition, analysing and commenting upon the advantages and disadvantages of holidays at home and abroad.

Practice 6

Specimen examination question

Paper 2, Section B: Writing to analyse, review, comment

Question 2
Some people prefer to live in towns and others prefer the countryside. A national magazine for teenagers is interested in the views of younger people and has asked for contributions from its readers.

Write your article, analysing and commenting upon the advantages and disadvantages of town and country life.

Check your answers

1   When you have completed your answers to each specimen question:

    a)   check that you have satisfied all the assessment objectives for writing (see page viii)

    b)   look at the mark scheme for writing on page xi – have you demonstrated the skills required to achieve a mark in the middle range?

2   If your teacher marks your answer, consider his or her comments and your mark. Is your mark in the middle range? Can you see why?

3   Consider what you could do to improve your mark, if you need to.

Glossary

Links to the assessment objectives on page viii are printed in purple.

Advise If your aim is to advise, you will offer evidence about what will happen in certain circumstances and make a recommendation for people to act upon.

Alliteration The deliberate repetition of a consonant sound for effect, usually the first letter, for example, *the slippery snake slid stealthily sideways*.

Analogy A comparison with something similar which is used to give the reader a clear idea of what the writer is saying. For example, 'sometimes they *spun languorously*, reminding me of the *lazy way smoke used to rise* from my father's pipe when he was reading'.

Analyse *(Reading)* To examine in detail, to take a close look at, to see which words were chosen and why. *(Writing)* To show that you can make comparisons, that you can point out the advantages and disadvantages of a particular course of action or of a particular state of affairs.

Anecdote A story used to illustrate a point.

Aphorism A short saying which expresses a general truth; also known as a maxim. Examples: *A man can't be too careful in the choice of his enemies. The only thing that interferes with my learning is my education. It's one thing to know the truth, and another to speak it.*

Argue If your purpose is to argue, you will need to have a clearly defined point of view, evidence to support it and some general, wider considerations to present on the topic.

Assonance The deliberate repetition of a vowel sound for effect, usually but not necessarily the first letter, for example, *amber apples hung above the arches*.

Audience The person or people who the writer intends will read a piece of writing.

Cliché A phrase which is over-used and has lost its impact, for example, *live and let live, over the moon, things will get worse before they get better.*

Comment To give your own point of view.

Compound words Words made by joining two normally unrelated nouns together (usually by using hyphen) to make a striking picture, or image.

Effective language The way we make the most of words.

Evaluate To make a judgement about, to assess, to appraise whether or not something is successful, effective, helpful, generally good – and why.

Fact Something which is real, which actually happened, which is true. Facts can be shown or demonstrated, for example, *It is a fact that Britain has a railway system.* (Assessment objective ii: Reading)

Genre The different types of writing which have their own features, for example travel writing, crime writing, historical writing, newspaper reports, biography.

Hyperbole Exaggeration.

Imagery The use of vivid language to create pictures in the reader's mind, for example by using **simile** or **metaphor**.

Language The way we express ourselves through words.

Linguistic features/devices These include **rhetorical questions**, lists, command, ironic statements, satire and humour, quoting from experts, officials, spokespersons and referring to scientific or other 'authorities'. (Assessment objective v: Reading; Assessment objective ii: Writing)

Metaphor When a writer writes about something as if it is something else so you see it in a new way.

Onomatopoeia The technique of using a word which actually sounds like the action it describes, for example, *snap, crackle and pop*.

Opinion A belief, a feeling, an idea, an impression, a point of view. Opinions may be strongly held and they may be based on good reasons; but they are *not* facts, for example, *In my opinion, Britain's railway system is very good!* (Assessment objective ii: Reading)

Persuade If your purpose is to persuade, you will need to present **facts** and **opinions** which will change somebody else's point of view, or change their actions or get them to do something.

Presentational devices/features The different ways the material is presented visually – the way it looks, the positioning of the text and illustrations. The text is all of the writing, and the illustations include photographs, cartoons, graphs, tables and charts. The editor *arranges* them in such a way as to make them most interesting and engaging to the reader. (Assessment objective v: Reading)

Register The different ways we speak or write to different kinds of people. You may write in a very formal way, or in a very elaborate, descriptive way, or sometimes your writing may be chatty, informal, more like everyday spoken language. The use of slang and colloquialism is part of register, as is dialect. Consider, for example, the way you speak to your friends at school and the way you speak to your grandparents.

Review By asking you to review an event or situation, the examiner is asking you to take a very close look at it – literally, to look at it again, with a close critical eye.

Rhetorical question A question which does not require an answer. It is a *rhetorical device*, a way of trying to persuade your audience to do or believe something. It is a verbal trick – a statement is framed as a question so the listener is drawn into thinking that his opinion is being sought. (*Rhetoric* (an Ancient Greek term) is the art of persuasive speaking or writing.) *See also* **Linguistic features/devices**

Simile When a writer compares one thing with another using the words 'as' or 'like' to link them.

Structural devices/features The different ways the writing can be put together (constructed) for different purposes/audiences, for example, using different length paragraphs for effect, different length sentences for emphasis or information, indentation, bullet points, bold type face and effective headings and sub-headings. The overall shape of the writing, how and where ideas are presented and developed is also a structural device. The main argument or point of view may not, for example, be at the beginning. (Assessment objective v: Reading; Assessment objective iii: Writing)

Tone The mood of a piece of writing – it tells us of a writer's attitude towards his or her subject, for example serious, light-hearted, angry or sad.

Other terms used in the assessment objectives

'Read, with **insight** and **engagement**' (Assessment objective i: Reading)
This really means that you should focus carefully on the text so that you understand it.

- To have **insight** means to understand what it really means.
- To **engage** means to connect with.

'**developing** and **sustaining** interpretations' (Assessment objective i: Reading)
This means that you need to show that you understand what the writer is getting at. You need to begin your interpretation (*develop* it) and make sure it fully answers the question (that it is *sustained*):

- To **develop** means to begin, commence.
- To **sustain** means to keep going.

'follow an **argument**, **identifying implications**' (Assessment objective iii: Reading)

- An **argument** means a point of view or several points of view.
- **Implication** means what else does the writer think will happen; what are the side effects?
- **Identifying** means reading the text carefully and finding the side effects.

'**select** ... and **collate material** from **different sources**, and **make cross-references**' (Assessment objective iv: Reading)

- To **collate** means to put texts next to each other and compare them.
- To **select material** means to choose appropriate information or quotations from the articles to use in your answer.
- **Different sources** means the two articles being compared.
- To **make cross-references** means to see what is similar or different between the two texts.

'communicate **clearly** and **imaginatively**' (Assessment objective i: Writing)

- **Clearly** means that you should avoid confusing your reader.
- **Imaginatively** means you need to keep your **audience** interested in what you are writing.

'using and adapting forms for **different readers and purposes**' (Assessment objective i: Writing)
To do this you need to think about your **audience** and the **register** you use (see definitions above).